The Teen's Guide to
Debating and
Public Speaking

The Teen's Guide to

Debating

and

Public Speaking

CLAIRE DUFFY

DUNDURN
PRESS

Library and Archives Canada Cataloguing in Publication

Duffy, Claire
[Australian schoolkids' guide to debating and public speaking]
    The teen's guide to debating and public speaking / Claire Duffy.

Originally published under title: The Australian schoolkids' guide to
    debating and public speaking.
Issued in print and electronic formats.
ISBN 978-1-4597-4178-2 (softcover).--ISBN 978-1-4597-4179-9 (PDF).--
ISBN 978-1-4597-4180-5 (EPUB)

    1. Public speaking--Juvenile literature. 2. Debates and debating--
Juvenile literature. 3. Reasoning--Juvenile literature. I. Title. II. Title:
Australian schoolkids' guide to debating and public speaking.

PN4121.D84 2018   j808.5'1   C2018-901302-8
                                               C2018-901303-6

We acknowledge the support of the Canada Council for the Arts and the Ontario Arts Council for our publishing program. We also acknowledge the financial support of the Government of Canada through the Book Publishing Industry Development Program and The Association for the Export of Canadian Books, and the Government of Ontario through the Ontario Book Publishers Tax Credit program and the Ontario Media Development Corporation.

Care has been taken to trace the ownership of copyright material used in this book. The author and the publisher welcome any information enabling them to rectify any references or credits in subsequent editions.   — J. Kirk Howard, President

The publisher is not responsible for websites or their content unless they are owned by the publisher.

Printed and bound in Canada.

Dundurn Press
Toronto, Ontario, Canada
dundurn.com, @dundurnpress

To E. and M. G.-S.
and the memory of
James the dog

Contents

Part 2: Public Speaking

Introduction

Welcome! I am delighted that you're reading this book, and that you plan to master the "mysterious" arts within it.

My own debating and public speaking career started in my first year at high school. I hadn't made it into a sporting team (then or ever, as it turned out) so I tried out for a public speaking competition. At the end of my speech the teacher leaned across the desk, and, frowning at the twelve-year-old me, said I was one of the best speakers she'd ever heard. It's possible I was the only speaker she'd ever heard (no one else was trying out), but the flattery worked. I was hooked.

It was practically the Pleistocene era. In those days you could *do* debating and public speaking at school, but neither of them was taught. We had to figure it out for ourselves. On Fridays my debating team used to squash into the back of a teacher's car to get to schools nearby, where we lost a lot. Eventually we learned that our opponents were being coached — by the adjudicator! (There was only one in our whole region.) So who knew if we were really any good or not. I left school thinking we might have been hopeless, and I was much too nervous to try university debating.

My interest flared again as a mom. My daughter loved debating. Well, "loved" is a bit of an understatement. You couldn't stop her. For years the high point of our family's week was debating, with added thrills if a public speaking competition was on. These were exciting times. We livened up, had a focus, and an interest we all shared. We became very good at arguing with each other. We made friends with the parents and kids from other schools who shared the same passion. My daughter's horizons expanded through learning how the world works, and thinking about what's right and good, and what's not and why. She went to new places and met new people. I enjoyed it so much that I asked her school principal if they could use any help, and the answer was yes. Pretty soon I was coaching a group of grade elevens. Soon I was coaching junior teams as well, and then I was coaching in several schools, and *then* I was in charge of a whole competition, working with dozens of people to make sure that debating was the highly valued and enjoyable experience it can be. Now it's my full-time job.

Meanwhile, my daughter became very, very good at it. She represented Australia in both debating and public speaking, and she's got a blazer with a gold Australian Coat of Arms on the pocket (you need the prime minister's okay for that!). At the World Schools Debating Championships, she and her team were ranked as the top four speakers in the world.

Introduction

These days, you don't take up debating and public speaking because you're no good at sports; it's cool to be one of the "speaky" kids, and it's organized properly. Anywhere in your country you can take part in a well-run competition. Most schools have dozens of students in debating. Oral presentations happen in class all the time, and for the more enthusiastic, there are external public speaking competitions. Adjudicators are trained, and a network of teachers and coaches help you get to a high standard.

As a parent and a teacher I know that debating and public speaking are the gateway to great enrichment, not just for you but for those around you. What you learn will include some of the most important things you ever learn. You will love exploring big issues, seeing into real-life dilemmas, and exercising your powers of self-expression.

Debating is excellent brain training. It sharpens your wits, teaches you how to reason, to think on your feet, to explain and justify a position, and to scour somebody else's work for flaws. It helps you see that whatever your personal beliefs, there is merit in the two sides of most arguments, and you must be able to justify yours. You will use this ability often, from answering exam questions, to later in "real" life, when it will help you do well at university and in the workplace.

Public speaking gives you space to be an individual, to say things that are original and off the beaten track of the school curriculum. There is no need to prove a point or demonstrate that you know the answer to a question. You can follow your own interests and present issues just because they matter to you. You will gain confidence as you formulate your ideas and speak them aloud. It's a rare opportunity. Young people are not often given the freedom to say, "This is interesting because ..." or "We could fix this problem if we tried this ..."

Both these pastimes teach you to engage with an audience and present information in a way that people want to listen. Most adults wish they could do this! It's also great fun. You will feel a thrill as you get the hang of it.

If you feel unsure, take heart. Public speaking and debating can both be learned. At school you develop these skills in a safe, supportive environment. You are among your friends, family, and teachers, who all want you to do well. Some of you are future champions. Some of you are brave kids who'll learn to do something they thought they could not. All of you are going to find this an interesting road to travel on.

HOW THIS BOOK WORKS

We start with a close look at debating. The first section explains what debating is. Then you are introduced to the art of argument and logical reasoning. Next come the specific skills you need in order to be a school debater. Exercises and examples are laced throughout, so you can give it a go.

Later in the book we look at public speaking. What do all good speeches have in common? How do you prepare and deliver one? You'll find advice on how to prepare a speech for a competition or handle some of the other public speaking commitments that can come your way as a school student.

Good luck! This is an adventure that you are going to enjoy.

Part 1

DEBATING

1

Debating — Why Do It?

Debating is fun. There's no better way of learning to think critically and to think on your feet and express yourself. Through debating you can grow your confidence, become persuasive, and get to know the world outside. Debating also teaches teamwork, time management, and how to work under pressure. It has a lot of life lessons as well!

Debaters learn

- speaking — how to talk fluently;
- arguing, using reason and logic;
- listening — hearing and understanding;
- interpreting and assembling the parts of a case into a whole;
- arranging and structuring thoughts into a logical progression; and
- the art of losing.

It's a challenging pastime, not for everyone. If you're starting out, congratulations — you are brave! Debaters deserve support and encouragement, and they need lots of practice. Debate is something you learn by doing.

WHAT IS DEBATING?

A debate is an organized argument.

There are two teams. Each is *for* or *against* something. The something is called the topic, or the proposition, or the motion. The "yes" team can be called Affirmative, Government, or Proposition. The "no" team is Negative or Opposition. Most debate styles have teams of two but sometimes three people. Everyone speaks once, but some speak twice.

Either side could win, but one side *will* win. You cannot have a draw.

In debating you must do two things:

1. You must present constructive arguments that convince the adjudicator you are right.
2. You must use rebuttal to prove the other side is wrong.

In some ways debating is like tennis, except that instead of hitting a ball backwards and forwards, you play with points of argument. A tennis player hits the ball over the net and gets it in. Their opponent returns it. Back and forth it goes, over and over the net, till someone hits a shot too good for the other person to return and they win.

Debaters make points to support their side of the argument, and their opponents have to rebut them. "Rebut" is debaterspeak for disprove or counteract. If you don't rebut your opponent's points, they win. If you do rebut them and make indestructible points of your own, you win.

HOW IT WORKS

As with any team, the people in it have roles to play. Each member has to do their bit, so that in the end all the bits fit together neatly — like a jigsaw puzzle — creating a case that is complete.

Each person is responsible for specific parts of the debate. The judge of the debate is the **adjudicator** (not the duplicator, as I was once called). They look at three things:

1. Matter or **content**: what you say, how relevant it is, whether it's logical, well-reasoned, and convincing.
2. Method or **strategy**: how well the speeches fit together to form a whole, the structure of your individual speeches, your rebuttal technique.
3. Manner or **style**: voice, face, eyes, body, gesture, use of notes. How interesting you are to listen to.

RULES AND JUDGING

Compared with other games and sports, the rules of debating are a bit softer and more open to interpretation. There can't be a photo finish or a video replay, and we don't have penalties, yellow cards, or sin bins. There isn't even a rule book to refer to. Though there are well-understood conventions for how a debate works, judging it involves art as well as science.

The adjudicator, or judge, scores the debate on how strong the arguments are, and how well each side destroys their opposition. They look at how well the team constructs a case and rebuts their opponents' overall, across all speakers. They judge according to what is actually said — no more, no less.

An adjudicator should not let their own views influence them. Weirdly, they won't find fault if you include errors of fact — the opposition has to do that — and they won't fill in the things you didn't quite say (even though you meant to).

There's some personal judgement involved here. Judges stick to a set of agreed approaches about what is important in a debate, but the fact is that they may see it differently from you. They have personal perspectives, as we all do.

When you lose, it's sometimes tempting to blame the adjudicator — they must be crazy if you lost. Well, maybe they *are* from another planet. But if so, they've given you a wonderful opportunity to learn something. Not getting what you hoped for is one of those things that will happen to you sooner or later, and going down gracefully is a skill you are going to need in life. If you have the guts to do debating, you have the guts to be the loser, even when it feels unfair.

The more elite you become as a debater, the larger the panel of adjudicators who will judge you. This is how major competitions reduce the influence of personal judgement over the result. Meantime, accept that sometimes an adjudicator will have only half the room agreeing with their decision!

WHAT ARE WE FIGHTING FOR?

You are probably quite used to arguing. You do it any time there's a disagreement about something you want. Going out on a school night? Extra time for your homework? Not to be sent out when you've mucked up in class?

To win these arguments you might stamp and scream, have a meltdown, play deaf, yell and slam doors, or throw the teacher a filthy look as you flounce out. (It wasn't *your* fault!)

In a debate, these approaches don't work. In a debate you are given a two-sided issue, and you must make points and use reasons and examples which fit logically together to make a case.

Debates are about genuine, real-life issues that people

don't agree on: Should our country take in more refugees? Should kids under the age of eighteen be banned from taking part in reality TV shows? Should parents get the blame if children break the law? There wouldn't be a debate if there was an obvious right side.

In real-life arguments and essays at school, you explain and justify your own point of view. You have an interest in the outcome — it will make a real difference to you. As a debater, however, you don't get to speak up for what you believe. Your side of the debate is decided by the toss of a coin. You have to be able to argue for or against it, regardless of your own views.

It is hard to argue for things you don't agree with. Powering into a fight, fired by the force of your feelings, is one thing; but in a debate, convictions are not much use. You have to find a way to argue *despite* your own opinion, not because of it.

When you argue in favour of something that you don't truly believe, it will teach you a lot. You'll be able to see that most sides of most arguments have points in their favour, and you'll learn not to assume people who disagree with you are idiots. (This is something many adults have yet to learn.) You might come to see the issue in ways you never did before. You will learn to think in a quick and organized way about some of the most important questions of your life and times.

It's one of the reasons I'm pleased you are reading this book. In real life, if you can see a problem from the opponent's side, there's a better chance of solving it. I'm not going to bring about world peace, but now you've bought this book, maybe one of you will.

2

The Art of Arguing

WHAT IS ARGUMENT?

Debate as we know it probably started with the ancient Athenians, who believed that orderly free speech was an important part of good government. For a man to be considered suitable for public leadership (sorry, girls, they didn't want you) he had to persuade people using reason. Not bribery or a knife at the throat, just reason, in the form of well-crafted, logical arguments. He was judged on this. Today it is still a sign of an intelligent, well-educated person that they reason things out in a systematic and logical way.

Note that I say "logical" and not "persuasive." The two are related but also quite different. Persuasion depends a lot on emotions. When we are stirred up and our feelings are engaged, we are more likely to take action, or change our minds about something.

Consider advertising. It's all about emotional appeal and the "Wow!" factor: gorgeous images, catchy songs, and promises to make you rich/thin/fit/beautiful. Advertising excites you, and before you can say "Think!" you are parting with your money. Or maybe you've been fired up by the persuasive powers of a speaker for a cause: the environment, a charity, medical research. After they'd finished, you were ready to help out in any way you could. That person was persuasive. In life you can be very successful if you can persuade people emotionally — but this is not what debating is about.

Arousing people's feelings won't hurt but it doesn't win a debate for you. Debates are about the mind, not the heart. When we talk about something being "persuasive" in debaterspeak, we mean that it's logical, compelling, and convincing.

The kind of arguments you will need are summarized in this table:

CLEAR	Not confusing
ACCURATE	True and able to be checked
PRECISE	Specific enough for the issue
RELEVANT	Important to the issue
BROAD	Able to accommodate other points of view
DEEP	Able to deal with complexity and complications
LOGICAL	Well-reasoned

This table is adapted from the critical thinking work of Linda Elder and Richard Paul.

HOW IT WORKS: INTRODUCING LOGIC, PREMISES, AND FALLACIES

If you were a doctor, you'd need to know how the human body works before you could go poking around in anybody else's. In the same way, you'll be a better debater if you understand what goes into a good argument and how they work. Understanding the shape of arguments will help you attack your opponents' weaknesses and defend your own position.

Logic

Forget passion, conviction, or fervent beliefs. Above all, the tools of debating are logic and reason.

Logical argument needs a cool head. Step by step, thinking clearly, you assemble a series of facts, beliefs, assumptions, or opinions. You arrange them so that one leads sensibly to another, and in the end you reach a conclusion — just like the answer to a sum. You have built a beautiful, logical case.

LOGICAL LANGUAGE

Every time a debater says "so" or "therefore" or "because," that is a sign they are making a logical argument. You need to use these words a lot.

Logic is a natural skill that you practise all the time. You use logic when you decide whether to walk or wait when you've missed the bus; when you play reasoning games, do puzzles, experiments, or maths problems; or when you try and figure out the answer to a mystery. You're already a logical thinker.

In everyday language we use "logical" to mean an argument is well-reasoned and convincing. But logic is also a formal subject of study, a branch of philosophy. Logicians study the process of reasoning. They break it down to discover the structure — how the different bits of an argument work together, like machine parts. Then they rewrite the argument using symbols, as if it was a mathematical equation.

In the formal study of logic, what makes an argument "valid" is its structure — the way it is built up. It's not necessarily important that the final answer is true.

This stuff does my head in, so don't worry if you're feeling confused too. We don't need to become logicians, but we need to understand just enough about logic to know that it is a big part of debating.

Premises

Logical arguments start with a premise (there can be more than one) and end with a conclusion. The person presenting the argument wants you to believe the conclusion on the basis of the premises. The premise is like the concrete slab that supports a house. It has to be a strong foundation, because everything that follows in the debate is built on it. A sound premise is very hard to argue with because — well, it's sound. It is understood that there is enough evidence and reason behind it to make it strong.

MS. DUFFY'S TOP TIP
One of your debating jobs is to hunt down weak or false premises and challenge them. If the premise is weak or false, the argument it supports will fall apart.

Finding the Premise

In debates it can be hard to find the premises. In some arguments they may not even be stated. You may hear the phrase "the underlying premise" or "the hidden assumption," which means that it hasn't been spoken aloud in the debate but is clearly under there. While locating the premise of an argument can be challenging, doing so will transform your arguments, and your debates will be much more substantial.

You have to think back and back or deeper and deeper to understand the assumptions that are hidden behind the issue of the debate.

Imagine someone telling you, "It's important for young people to do debating because it teaches them how to argue." The conclusion is clear: "It's important for young people to do debating." One of the premises is visible, too: "Debating teaches you how to argue." But arguing might be a useless or undesirable skill. There's a *hidden* assumption that "learning to argue is important."

To find the premise, you need to ask what idea or belief an argument is resting on. Say something like "That argument assumes ..." and your answers will help you see what the premise is.

You might be surprised at how many premises are contentious (this means they can be debated). Try looking for the premises in everyday arguments and then questioning them. When Mom tells you to do your homework, the premise of her argument is that doing homework is good. Why? Is it because it's good for your brain? Because you'll get punished if you don't? If homework wasn't good for you, would she still want you to do it? Find out if *she* knows ...

In a debate about excluding smokers from coverage by health care, for example, the Proposition will say something like, "Smoking is very bad for your health and if people choose to hurt themselves, they should bear the costs of treatment — it's not the government's fault they made themselves sick, so fixing it should not cost the government money."

One of their premises is that health care (government help) is only for people who "deserve" it.

The Opposition will say that health care exists to care for the health of all of us, even people who do not make sensible lifestyle choices.

One of their premises is that health care (government help) is universal, for everyone.

Watch out for premises. Often one of them will be the point on which the debate turns. Thinking through an argument to identify its premise is really important if you are going to build a logical case from it.

NOW YOU KNOW The most important part of debating is argument, and the most important part of argument is being logical and convincing. Good arguments are based on sound premises, even if they are hidden. Check the assumptions in an argument to be sure they are correct.

What Is a Fallacy?

You can be a good debater without knowing the word "fallacy," but you will understand the art of argument much better if you learn about it.

A fallacy is an argument that doesn't work. However convincing it feels, it is tricking you. A debater has to be like a detective, on the hunt for the fallacies and holes. They reveal the weak spots in your opponent's (and your own) arguments.

Here is a famous, very simple form of argument to show you what I mean. Warning: it is booby-trapped.

All men are mortal.
James is mortal.
Therefore, James is a man.

Sound right? The two statements we started with and the conclusion seem to make a logical argument, especially if James is, let's say, my brother.

But suppose James is not my brother? Suppose James is my family dog. And she's female. (Yes, we have a girl dog with a boy's name.) Here she is.

Oops. We started off with two true statements, but the conclusion is false. So the argument must be illogical.

Here's the really tricky thing: it's not a fallacy *because* the conclusion is false. Even if James was my brother and the conclusion were true, the argument itself would still be flawed. You just can't draw that conclusion from those two statements.

It was a fallacy.

Unconvincing, illogical arguments are based on fallacies. If you like debating you will enjoy finding out more about different types of fallacies.

Fallacies — A Debater's Guide

Once the arguments are being presented, your job is to rebut them by finding their faults. Here is a list of some common fallacies — that is, ways of arguing illogically. You don't have to be able to remember all these straight away, and you don't have to call them by name in a debate, though it is pretty impressive if you do. The list is simply to help you understand the ways arguments can be flawed.

Red Herring

I do not know why herrings get the blame, but a red herring is when you distract attention from the main issue by bringing up something that's beside the point. The aim is to turn the debate in another, irrelevant direction.

CHECK YOUR ASSUMPTIONS

In our James-the-dog example there were two premises: that men are mortal and that James is mortal. Both were true, though the conclusion was false. If you assumed James was a man, that was fair enough. A thing called James usually is a man (or a boy, who will become a man). In this case, however, your assumption was false. There's a lesson in this, because an awful lot of things that we think are true turn out only to be based on what's usual. Once you know this, you can see that an awful lot of assumptions can be challenged.

In a debate about kids being on their computers too much, you might hear "Children today spend too much time on screens. In my Dad's day they used to run around for fun." What Dad used to do does not have any bearing on whether today's kids spend too much time on their computers. If you chase this red herring, you'll soon be comparing the good ol' days with now. That's not the topic!

Misrepresenting the Evidence

Evidence can easily be used to create a false conclusion. This is especially true in our media-soaked world, which serves up dramatic stories every few seconds. You might think plane crashes are constant, but take a look at the statistics. Because we hear about it when one happens, we get scared that it's unsafe to fly, when it may not be.

Watch out for debaters who do the same thing. Scary, lurid, frightening cases or examples stick in your mind, but question the facts behind the examples they put forward, and if they are distorting the truth, say so.

Cherry-Picking

This is when you use only information that works for your side, and ignore anything that contradicts your position. You distort the case by being selective about the evidence.

In a debate you will have to do a bit of this — but a smart debater uses "pre-emptive rebuttal" to acknowledge and dispose of the obvious arguments against them. (See the chapter on rebuttal starting on page 127.)

Straw Man

The "straw man" is a flimsy version of a real man, a figure made to be laughed at and destroyed. It refers to one side oversimplifying and misrepresenting the other side's idea so that it sounds ridiculous. For example, if you respond to "Parents should be able to monitor their children's online activities to help protect them from harm" by saying "So just because they are young, children are to have *no* independence or privacy?" you have created a straw man. It misrepresents the argument, and that is a shabby trick.

Slippery Slope

This is very common in school debates. The idea is that if we relax the rules and allow some sort of concession — a lower voting age, children to choose their own bed time, certain drugs to be legalized — it is the first step on the road to ruin. The downward slide is inevitable; if you start, you can neither stop nor turn back. (I'm sure you can tell already that this is not a convincing argument.)

For example: If we let children choose their own bed time, they will want to stay up as late as possible. In no time at all (the slippery slope argument goes) the streets will be overrun by kids who are out at all hours, mugging upright citizens, thieving and robbing, and clogging up the police stations after they've been arrested. "Early bed time for kids will keep our society safe!" the debater might say. The slippery slope creates a false connection between late bed time and bad behaviour. It's plainly not logical. A much better argument against allowing late nights for children would be to focus on the healthy need for growing bodies to get eleven hours of sleep a night. (Not to mention the need for their parents to get a few hours of peace and quiet at night when the kids are in bed.)

A "no health care for smokers" debate could be turned into a slippery slope. If we allow the government to keep smokers out of health care today, who's next? They could do the same to alcohol drinkers, the overweight, or people who don't wear sunscreen! Soon you will be excluded from health-care coverage if you don't cover your coughs or wash your hands before eating.

Some multi-step arguments are reasonable. There is evidence that obese adults often had poor eating habits when they were children. Eating too much sugar as a child really does start you on a path to adult obesity and its many health problems. On this basis you might justify banning junk food ads around children. "If we help young people eat good food and keep to a healthy weight, they are less likely to be obese later in their lives."

Generally speaking, take no more than a step or two down the slippery slope.

False Cause

This is when you suggest something has been caused by something but it hasn't really. Often it's because two things occur close in time. It looks as though one caused the other but it was only a coincidence. Let's say you got a new school principal, and then the school's results got better right away. It might be because of something the principal did or it might not; it might have happened anyway, regardless of who the principal was.

Are you superstitious? Did your favourite team win the day you wore a beanie to the game? If you wear that beanie to every game afterwards in the hope it will help your team win, you believe in a false cause.

Complex Cause

Complex causes are very common in debates. Nearly every problem that pops up as a debate topic has many causes. You should acknowledge this.

I may say, "Ban candy from the school cafeteria and prevent childhood obesity!" But it's not just the sweets that are causing obesity, so banning them is not going to fix it. Saying that it will is a fallacy. Obesity is caused by a range of things: eating too many calories, not doing enough exercise, being in a family or social group that does this, too, and so on. Banning sweets at school may help (and you can argue that it is important for the school to set a good dietary example), but it's unlikely to be a cure.

False Dilemma

Does it sound like a simple "either/or" choice, suggesting there are only two ways to go, when really there are other options? Does it sound like, "You're either with us or against us," when there may be another way? The false dilemma suggests that two things are clearly in opposition to each other and are the only choices, when the reality is there are more subtle options.

A "longer school day" debate might suggest extending classes past 3:00 p.m. on weekdays, but if we really want more in-school hours for students we could suggest opening schools on the weekend or shortening the holidays. There are more options than just staying back later than we already do.

Generalization

One example does not always prove a point. In a debate on the need to get more women into public life, someone might say, "There is no problem — we've had one female leader already." We're not arguing about whether it's possible; we're arguing that we need more. The existence of a small number of women in public life does not prove that we have enough.

Ad Hominem ("To the Person")

Also known as "playing the man, not the ball," this is when you attack the person's character instead of the issue. It's a kind of name-calling. You are saying that they automatically have a certain attitude or position on an issue because of who they are or where they come from — for example, "Someone from [your opponent's school] *would* say that!"

You hear ad hominem arguments all the time in politics: "Now this from the party who brought you

Fallacies aren't just easy traps for young debaters. Grown-ups make big mistakes in their jobs if they fall into a fallacy. Some common grown-up fallacies are ad hominem, appealing to popularity, and circular reasoning, but there are lots more. Listen for these on the news this week. Bonus points if you can catch a teacher.

that!" or "We know what an idiot s/he is." It does not prove anything. The person's character, or who they are, has no bearing on the validity of their ideas. It's not an argument, it's an insult. Don't do it.

Appealing to Popularity

You may think that if everybody follows an idea it must be good. Maybe but not always. Fast food is very popular — not good for you, though. Not so long ago it was popular to smoke. Everyone used to think the earth was flat. History is full of once popular ideas that are now a source of shame: slavery, child labour, not allowing women to vote, watching bears get eaten by dogs for fun. And some things may be popular in one place but not somewhere else. Communism, for example: a big hit in Russia and China; never caught on in the U.S. Being popular proves only that something is — well, popular.

Appeal to Authority

I'm not an expert on space travel or computer programming or how to bake brownies but there are people out there who are. I am prepared to believe what they tell me.

If a respected and knowledgeable person says something, we are likely to accept it. This is useful for debating, because you can use expert opinion as a form of evidence to support your point. Strictly speaking, though, it's a logical fallacy. Is something true just because someone says so? No. Can a famous scientist be wrong? Yes, of course.

As we know, though, debating is about convincing the adjudicator that something is likely to be the case. An expert's opinion will certainly carry weight, but it does not automatically seal the argument in your favour.

MS. DUFFY'S TOP TIP

If you want to use experts, be careful to choose good ones. Does that expert really know their stuff? They are useful to you only when their authority is legitimate or relevant.

Celebrities endorse products all the time. They get paid to do so. If a great runner endorses certain running shoes, that makes sense. But how about when Roger Federer, tennis champ, endorses a Rolex watch? Does playing excellent tennis make him a good judge of watches? Did having a good watch make any difference to his tennis? I can't see how. It's an effective promotional technique but as an argument for Rolex? Nope.

Appealing to Emotion

Instead of appealing to reason, an argument can arouse strong emotions. Advertising is one of the best examples. Ads promise to make you better, stronger, faster, prettier, fitter, slimmer ... and use fear, pity, and flattery to persuade you. These are emotional tactics, and they do not involve reason. They are therefore weak tools to win a debate with.

In the example above, Federer's endorsement works because, as well as being one of the best tennis players on the planet, Federer has charm, a nice family, and seems like he's someone you would get along with. He's more than a top-class tennis player, he's a top-class person — who would naturally make good choices when buying a watch (feel the illogicality coming on?). If you too choose a Rolex, you and Roger will have something in common. In fact, you must be a top-class person too. Mmmm ... I'm feeling good just thinking about it.

Argument From Silence

A lack of evidence does not mean something isn't true. You can't argue that something *isn't* true simply because there is no evidence to prove it. Not proven and disproven are different things. There is a difference between finding out for sure that something is not so and simply not knowing.

Is there life on other planets? There's no evidence but then again that would be hard to collect even if it existed, so the honest answer is "We're not sure."

Circular Reasoning

Also known as "begging the question," this is when the premise and the conclusion amount to the same thing. A circular argument starts from an assumption and ends with the same assumption. Sorry, folks, but an argument can't prove itself.

"That boat won't float because it will sink" is circular, whereas "That boat won't float because it has a hole in it" is better.

"Sports stars are role models because people want to be like them" is circular. "Sports stars are role models because they are elite leaders" is better.

"We must have harsher jail sentences because at the moment criminals are just getting community service orders" says the same thing twice. "We must have harsher jail sentences because we need to do more to deter people from crime" breaks the circularity and provides a real reason.

"Begging the question" does not mean begging to ask the question. It's an expression that's very commonly misused.

YOU'LL NEVER MAKE A PERFECT CASE

Debate topics aren't about facts. You can't ever prove them for sure. Instead, debates involve arguments for and against a certain idea, and either side can be "right."

Because of this, you won't ever make logically perfect, completely watertight arguments in debates. Your job is to puzzle out the most convincing way to argue a point of view about a real-life issue. You have to convince listeners that something could, might, or should be a good (or bad) idea.

We often say a bad argument has "holes." Ever heard someone say an argument doesn't hold water? That's because it has holes! Your arguments will have holes. Don't worry — so will your opponents'. Part of the fun is exposing the holes in their arguments while hiding the holes in yours.

GIVE IT A GO! You might enjoy being a trainee logician and exploring the difference between an argument being valid and its parts being true. Don't worry, you don't really need to know this detail for debating. Most of us have a pretty good nose for whether an argument has holes. But if you like puzzles you might find this is fun to play with, and it could give your debaterbrain a bit of extra power.

The really big rule is that if you have true premises and a valid argument the conclusion must be true. But what about these:

- Can you have true premises and an invalid argument?
- Can you have a valid argument and a false conclusion?
- If your argument is not valid, does that mean the conclusion must be false?

Try Googling "logical fallacies for young people." Have a look and see if you can understand the differences between the sound and the unsound. There are also some fun examples on the website Truth of Statements, Validity of Reasoning: legacy.earlham.edu/~peters/courses/log/tru-val.htm.

THE PERSUASIVE POWER
OF REASONS

Reasons are essential to any logical argument. Reasons justify your argument. They say why your viewpoint is convincing. Good, strong reasons help the listener settle in and accept what you say. They are like streetlights at night, illuminating the road and making it easy for your audience to go along with you.

Reasons require you to use the word "because."

Let's consider an everyday debate, the kind of argument that happens at home all the time, a typical parent/child scenario. You want to do something and the resident adult does not want you to.

You say, "Mom, I'm going out tonight, even though it's a school night." Well, no, at this stage, I'd say you're not.

How about instead you say, "Darling Mother, I'm going out tonight, a school night, because I have done all my homework and there is nothing on TV worth staying home for, only *The X-Factor* and *Junior Master-Chef Meets Survivor.*"

The "B" word is there, so you've given a reason. Good start.

Your mother may say, "Okay, dear, don't be late." More likely she will say, "That's great, because you're now available to do the dishes, feed the dog, tidy your room, fold the laundry, and mind your little sister. I can get to my metalwork class on time for once!"

You should get used to giving reasons all the time. Say "because" and "this matters because" whenever you can in daily life.

Your reason wasn't strong. Your mom spotted its weakness and turned it to her advantage. You're staying home.

In debating, you win if your reasons are hard to argue with. If your reason is strong, your opponent can't **rebut** you (that's debaterspeak for "argue against").

Watertight Reasons

How do you make a strong reason? The key is to justify your opinion in a way that does not start more arguments.

Begin with a bit of crystal ball gazing. Look at what an opponent is likely to say to get back at you, and make sure you've prepared an answer. Better still, make your reason so good they never express their opposition in the first place.

If you'd thought about this issue from your mom's point of view, you would have realized right away where her interests are. She has a long list of chores and responsibilities that she would like some help with. Then you, being smart, might have said, "It's okay for me to go out on a school night, Mother dear, because I've done all my homework, and I can do some chores for you and take Zoe to the neighbours' place on my way out. Why don't you hurry off to metalwork? I promise to tidy my room tomorrow." You've taken care of her objections before she even had a chance to make them. In the debating world, this is called **pre-emptive rebuttal**.

Reasons and explanations are still more convincing if they will put an end to something that is harmful and produce a result that is beneficial. Say what good things will result, and also talk about the harms that are cured by it.

It's much harder for your mom to say no if she thinks keeping you home will actively hurt you. Suppose you'd said, "I would like to go out tonight, Mother dear. Even though it's a school night, all my friends are going to the game to support our friend Elphabar, who's in the team. It's a group thing. If I don't go they might think I don't care about them and I'll (voice cracking with emotion) become a social outcast." Mothers hate their children suffering for even a nanosecond. She doesn't want you to be unhappy. You've made it clear that it's good for you if she lets you go, and that you might suffer some social damage if she does not. Get your coat — you're on the way to the game!

To win a debate, your reasons have to be good. Good reasons can't be easily rebutted. The best reasons put an end to something harmful. If whatever you're saying is true, observable, and stops something nasty, it is more convincing.

How to Become a Reason Machine

You should get into the habit of giving reasons all the time. Say "Because ..." and "This matters because ..." at every opportunity.

"I'd like more calorific-sugar-loaded-choco-breakfast-junk-food please, because I don't have enough to fill me up. This matters because my mood will be foul if I go to school hungry."

"Can I borrow your charger, please, because I foolishly forgot mine. This matters because I need to call home and I have no battery."

"I would like to enrol in karate classes, because I enjoy moving with balance and precision, and the skill of knocking people over is one I would like to develop. This matters because I am sick of being a loser."

Everyday domestic disputes offer excellent training opportunities. Honing your skills on issues of personal importance is a good way to go — anything from your bedtime, to eating your vegetables, to where to take vacations, or what subjects you choose to study. All offer great opportunities for practising giving reasons and explaining why they are important. Try it and see if it improves your success rate.

If you have a teacher who is a good sport, try persuading her or him not to assign homework one day. Explain that it is a debating exercise so they don't think you're just being pushy; they will appreciate that it is a vital part of your development.

Using Evidence and Proof

Evidence exists outside, in the real world. It's those little bites of reality that illustrate what you're saying and make it feel true. Without evidence, your arguments may sound like good ideas but that's all.

Evidence shows that what you're saying is not just your own opinion. Because it is available to anyone, people could check it out and decide for themselves whether what you are saying is reasonable.

Your evidence doesn't have to be scientifically proven, but it does have to be believable, trustworthy information. It's alright to rely on common knowledge and expert opinion in a debate, the kind of thing a well-informed person would be aware of.

Student debaters sometimes think that numbers offer instant proof. If you do happen to know some figures to support your argument, by all means use them, but in a school debate it is acceptable to say "many" or "most" or "there has been a dramatic rise/fall in ..." or even "it's reasonable to think that ..."

The evidence needs to prove what you are saying is generally true. One or two instances may not be real proof.

MS. DUFFY'S TOP TIP

Using multiple examples strengthens your case. A well-explained point with one example to support it is good, but a point with three examples is much more convincing.

If your mother said, "No way are you going to any game! Josh Jeldbridge was picked up by the *police* there last Thursday night!" she is using a single instance (which no doubt has a lot more to it) to prove your idea is a bad one. She's distorting things, generalizing from one case. The evidence should belong to a general pattern. If a whole lot of kids were getting into trouble with the police, it'd be a different story.

It would be great if you could tell your mother that there is evidence that socializing on school nights improves academic performance, but sadly for you, such evidence probably does not exist. You could, however, say, "C'mon, Ma — lots of kids go to the game every week and it isn't hurting their marks so far."

Using multiple bits of evidence strengthens your case still more. A well-explained point with one piece of evidence to support it is good, but a point with three instances is starting to be very weighty indeed.

Also remember that, though not ideal, a good argument supported by weak evidence can still be a good argument.

NOW YOU KNOW The number one lesson in this chapter is that argument means being logical and giving good reasons. Good reasoning depends on asking yourself "Why?" and using the word "because" to justify what you're saying. Good reasoning also requires not falling into any of the fallacy traps, which are arguments that look and sound convincing but are really not.

GIVE IT A GO! Try these reasoning games.

Parachute

Name a small group of well-known people. They can be alive or dead, real or fictional. Mix them up, so, for example, world leaders are with movie stars, religious leaders, and sports heroes. They're on a plane that's about to crash and there's only one parachute. Who gets it? Who should be saved? Why? Argue for your character to get the parachute.

If I Ruled the World

The first person in the circle announces their name and makes a statement about what they would do if they ruled the world. They have to say why this is a good idea and what harm it will fix. For example:

"My name's Antonio and if I ruled the world, I would teach everyone to swim. Swimming is good exercise and not enough people do it. They are missing out on something special."

"My name is Sophia and if I ruled the world I would eliminate disease. Disease is causing millions of people to suffer and eliminating it will make all those millions happy."

Then add a second element — saying how you will do it.

"My name's Antonio and if I ruled the world, I would teach everyone to swim. Swimming is good exercise and not enough people do it. They are missing out on something special. I will offer to send teams of swimming teachers to all the governments of the world."

"My name is Sophia and if I ruled the world I would eliminate disease. Disease is causing millions of people to suffer and eliminating it will make all those millions happy. I will get the United Nations to make all the rich countries provide doctors, money, and assistance to all the poor countries."

Switch

Form a circle. One person, the controller, announces the topic, for example "We should make the school day longer," then points to another person and says "Switch," whereupon that second person has to start speaking, making an argument in favour. Every thirty seconds the controller points to a new person and says "Switch," with each new speaker continuing as if it were the same speech. After a while, the controller says "Change" and people have to start making arguments against the motion, with the controller pointing and switching randomly between speakers as before.

Argue With Me

Get your mom or dad or someone else to read aloud a short opinion piece from the news. Take notes as they speak. Then challenge what they said using the following formula: "You say that ... but I say that ... (make your point) because (give a reason and explanation)."

Crossing the Floor

After a discussion on any matter of opinion, get your group to show what side they're on by standing in one place if they agree and another place if they disagree. Every few minutes as the discussion continues, any "mind changers" should cross the floor to the new place. At the end, discuss the reasons that convinced people to switch.

3

How to Prepare a Case

TOPICS AND HOW TO TREAT THEM

The first thing you meet in a debate is the topic. You might think topics are the simplest part of the debate. WRONG. They're the most complicated.

A topic's sole purpose is to cause disagreement. You should feel interested, surprised, outraged, or upset when you get the topic. It's meant to stir you up.

To treat a topic properly, you have to take it apart and examine it, like a scientific specimen, in order to become very clear about what it means and why it's there in the first place. It's this deep thinking about the topic that is the first step to preparing a winning case.

Topics sound like a declaration. Imagine there's an exclamation mark at the end of each of these:

America should close its borders.

Off-road vehicles should not be allowed on suburban streets.

Computer games are doing more harm than good.

When you get the topic, ask yourself, "Does this topic want something to change?" If so, it's a "should" debate. If not, it's an "is" debate.

Young people should not use their real names online.
It is unfair to deceive children about the existence of Santa Claus.

The best topics are clear and don't cause confusion. It's easy to see the issue and that it has two sides. The point of the debate is obvious to both teams. Do you think that's true about the topics in the list above?

Interpreting Topics

Sometimes, the main issue in the debate is not quite clear — there is room to move. The words used in the topic are a bit "non-exact." Before you can debate, you and your team have to agree among yourselves what the words are supposed to mean and what the debate is really about. You need to interpret or explain the topic.

Your interpretation of the topic is like the soil your case grows from. It has to be prepared well so that it is rich, sustaining, and packed full of nutrients. Leaving some little thing out will weaken it.

If you are the Proposition, you will be defining the topic and you may have to decide between a few possible approaches. To do that, follow these four steps:

1. Look at the topic. Hard.
2. Underline the key words.
3. Circle any words which might have mixed or hidden meanings — words that are debatable.
4. Paraphrase the topic, restate it into your own words, then share.

With two team brains at work on the same topic, you might be surprised how many different ways this issue can be looked at. This is useful because it gives clues as to what the other side may come up with when they argue against you. Here's a worked example:

The debate should be about protecting vulnerable people who are too young to make their own decisions, so let's say <15.

YOUNG PEOPLE (SHOULD) NOT USE THEIR REAL NAMES ONLINE

Do we want there to be a penalty if they do, or is this just about what's best for them?

The names on their ID documents & any nicknames that would identify them.

We want this debate to be interesting, and not bogged down in practicalities like "what if kids need to order books online?" So let's limit "online" to mean social media e.g. Facebook, Instagram.

IN MY OWN WORDS! *kids should have to use fake usernames when they use social media sites.*

If you then have to decide between a few possible approaches, ask yourselves the following:

- Which will create more disagreement? Choose the one that leads to the most heated argument, not the one that's easiest to win.
- Which is fairest for the other team? What would they be expecting? Don't interpret topics in a way that would surprise a normal person. That's not fair. Don't twist the topic to mean something it wasn't intended to.
- Which interpretation is easiest to express? Make it clear and strong. "We interpret 'peace' to mean no more military fighting, but we don't mind if there are still religious or verbal disagreements between countries and cultures."

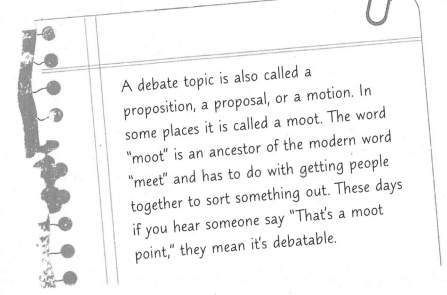

A debate topic is also called a proposition, a proposal, or a motion. In some places it is called a moot. The word "moot" is an ancestor of the modern word "meet" and has to do with getting people together to sort something out. These days if you hear someone say "That's a moot point," they mean it's debatable.

Types of Topics

Debates come in three categories:

1. **Facts:** Is something true?
2. **Policies:** What we should do about something.
3. **Values:** Matters of judgement.

In school debates you don't usually get "type 1" topics, so you won't have to argue about whether something is, indeed, a fact. If you want to do this professionally, become a lawyer and argue this way in court.

Although you don't debate whether something is a fact, you do need facts and information. It's the story told by those facts that you can interpret and present in your own way.

"Should" Topics

"Type 2" topics say what "should" be the case. For example:

We should ban smoking.

The U.N. should have its own army.

We should limit tourism at the Grand Canyon.

These topics want some sort of action, something to be done differently. The Proposition has to say, "Yes, do it!" and the Opposition has to say, "No, do nothing — or at least don't do what the other team wants."

To debate these you need to supply a reason for change and say that this particular change will do more good than the harm of leaving things as they are (which is called the status quo).

You must give reasons for making the change, and you should present a plan of how to do it. (More on all of this later.)

"Is" Topics

"Type 3" topics are debates that involve a judgement about what is the case:

Space exploration is a waste of money.
We are better off than our grandparents were.

Here you must argue a point of view, realizing that the idea of "harm" or "better off" or "waste of money" is not clear-cut. What these terms mean to you will be different from what they mean to me.

To have this debate you must think about what "harm" and "good" and "waste of money" actually look like. How would we know if we had them or not? Sometimes these are called yardstick debates. A yardstick is an old-fashioned ruler. You need a standard, something to measure by.

In some debates the topic starts with the words "This house would ..." This is a hangover from the parliamentary origins of debating. The "house" refers to Parliament.

INTRODUCING STAKEHOLDERS

"Stakeholders" is debaterspeak for people affected by the issue. Knowing who they are and how they're affected helps you develop a well-rounded debate and usually gives you some easy material for your third and fourth points: How are the stakeholders affected by the proposed solution? Does it make their life harder or easier?

Consider who they are and in what way they are affected, both by the current situation and by the changes your team proposes.

HOW TO START YOUR CASE PREP

When you have your topic and you know what the debate is going to be about, you need to get started on your case. That's debaterspeak for your argument, the story your team tells to prove your side is right.

To make a case you will present a series of points. A point is like a brick or a building block. When stacked up and connected in a logical and convincing way, you have a strong case.

You need at least four, maybe five, points in a case. Normally the first speaker presents two or three points, and the second speaker gets one or two (depending on the style of debate and how many speakers you have, these numbers may shift). Opposition teams need only four points, since they use more of their time on rebuttal.

MS. DUFFY'S TOP TIP

The most important points — the ones that your side must prove to win the debate — always go to the first speaker.

Imagine you are an architect, not a builder. Your first job is to do a sketch plan. You want to design and outline a general shape — the details of your case come later. All you need now is a set of headlines, a bit like chapter titles in a book. Think of them as the skeleton that supports a body.

In this section we go through how to prepare a case for either "should" or "is" topics.

PREPARING "SHOULD" TOPICS

"Should" topics say there should be a change. You need two types of arguments to win a "should" debate. You have to prove that what your team says is the right thing (moral) and that it will work (practical). You should prove both of them.

Your case should also prove your opposition's proposal is wrong and that it won't work. In other words,

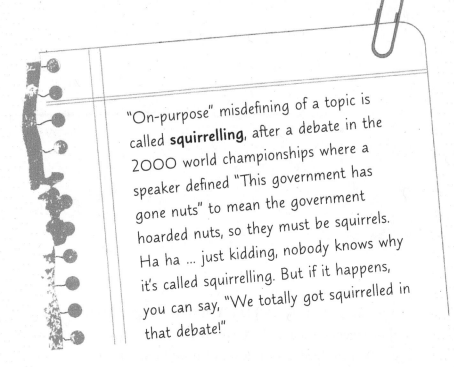

"On-purpose" misdefining of a topic is called **squirrelling**, after a debate in the 2000 world championships where a speaker defined "This government has gone nuts" to mean the government hoarded nuts, so they must be squirrels. Ha ha ... just kidding, nobody knows why it's called squirrelling. But if it happens, you can say, "We totally got squirrelled in that debate!"

it's immoral and impractical. But before you can do that, we need to start with some basics.

There are several steps to go through:

- You need a topic definition.
- You must explain the problem and provide evidence in support.
- You have to come up with a plan/solution/plan of action.
- You need to argue some points.

Preparing the Proposition is different from preparing the Opposition, so we are going to look at each side of the debate separately.

Proposition

Defining the Topic

On the Proposition side, your first speaker defines the topic. It's one of the good things about being on the Proposition. You own the topic. You get to interpret it, you tidy up its inexactness, and YOU decide what it means. You can trim it into shape — like a hedge.

You don't need a dictionary, just a common sense explanation of what the topic means as a whole. Never deliberately fiddle with the definition and twist it to mean something when it really doesn't.

Here are some questions you should ask yourself when you're doing the definition:

1. Who Are "We" Anyway?

If your debate topic uses the word "we," you have to clear up who that is. The "we" is whoever would take the action your topic calls for. It could be a person, or a group of people, an institution, or organization. It's often the government but can also be some other body that's in charge of something.

Ask yourself, Who can make the change happen? Who has the authority, the ability, and also the right? Some examples:

- We should ban the gas engine (government).
- We should allow the internet to be available during exams (school principal).
- We should allow parents access to their children's online activity (Hmmm … this one's tricky. How *could* parents get this?).

2. What Is the Most Important Word in the Topic?

Work out what the most important word in the topic is and make sure you are defining it in a way that an ordinary person would agree with. Definitions are not supposed to make your own points easier — they are supposed to make the debate topic clear. If there is a word like "drugs," "bullying," or "charity," which not everyone would understand the same way, you can specify what you want that word to mean in the debate. Just make sure you're doing it to make the debate tidier for everyone, not easier for you.

3. What Are the Unimportant Words in the Topic?

Junior debaters sometimes over-define. If there are ordinary words or phrases like "child," "school," "junk food," or "money" in the topic, you don't need to define them, because most people will understand them in the same way. You'll sound like you swallowed a dictionary if you define everything.

Explain the Problem

Once you've defined the topic, the next step is to identify the problem the "should" topic is trying to solve. Otherwise there's no reason for having the debate.

1. What's the Problem?

What is the problem we are trying to solve? The answer will give you the backbone to build the case around, and provide most of your points.

For example, if the topic is *We should limit tourism to the Grand Canyon,* the suggestion is that this will solve something — but what? Maybe it's the noise and pollution from air tours, cars, and buses; maybe it's that visitors introduce new plant and animal species that do damage to the environment and ecosystem; maybe it's that leaving the trails to look over the rim can be dangerous, and fewer tourists will mean fewer accidents and deaths; maybe it's to divert people to other tourist attractions and national parks in America (there are plenty!). Whatever the reason, you can't talk about why it's good to have fewer tourists at the canyon until you've been clear about the problem it's intended to fix.

2. What's the Harm?

When you've identified the problem, you need to do one more thing. You need to say why we should care about the problem. To do that, you need evidence that the problem causes harm. Stack on some examples! Let's say the topic was *Schoolchildren should be made to handwrite their homework*. The problem we're trying to solve is that schoolchildren have bad handwriting, but the Opposition could easily say, "Who cares if children have bad handwriting? Nobody uses handwriting much any more, and computer skills are more valuable for later life." In "should" debates you must convince them that solving the problem is a worthwhile thing to do.

The best way is to show that the harm will last as long as this problem goes unsolved. Maybe it harms individual people, the country's economy, our values and morals — it could be lots of things. The important thing is to explain why those harms matter. You must be able to say, "That's bad because …"

Sometimes this is easy. If the harm is clear-cut and terrible, like "Children will die unless we solve this problem," most people will agree. But sometimes, as in our handwriting example, you need to work harder to make sure that the end of the sentence "That's bad because …" is clear and persuasive. You'd need an example of evidence like: "Poor handwriting is bad for students because it means they aren't developing their fine motor skills, or learning to be tidy and methodical, or to take care with their written communications."

Let's say the topic is *We should stop health-care coverage for diseases caused by obesity*. You might say the problem is that "This country is the fattest in the world, and half our children are obese." We all know that obesity is unhealthy, but you still need to come out and say it. If the Proposition doesn't say what harm obesity is doing, the Opposition can say, "So what? Who cares? People can be fat if they like. Nothing needs to change."

So the Proposition must say why obesity is bad. "Obesity causes preventable deaths, especially from heart disease and diabetes. These hurt the individuals, their families, and eventually, as the numbers grow, put a strain on our whole hospital and health-care system. We can't keep up with the demand to treat people for illnesses they did not need to get in the first place."

PRO TIP

The harm doesn't have to mean the world will end. Don't be afraid to say "a few people will lose their jobs." That's bad enough. You don't have to say "and this will ruin their families' lives, and the economy will die, and our country will lose its standing in the world." That's exaggeration. It's not convincing and it's not necessary.

Ella, grade eleven

3. What's the Cause?

So far we've identified the problem and told people why they should care about it. The next step is to show how your team will solve it — but wait! Solving it involves explaining the cause. Aim to remove the cause, and you cure the problem at the same time.

Think of the reasons why the problem exists in the first place. Find the fit between the causes of the problem and your solution.

In "should" debates, the topic is already expressed as if it were a solution to a problem, and that means you need to work backwards from this solution and come up with causes that match the solution your topic has forced on you.

For instance, if the topic is *Schools should punish the parents of bullies,* you need to show that there's a link between parenting and bullying at school. Parents have to be part of the problem. Otherwise why would punishing them solve bullying? You will have to say that poor parenting creates bullies or that unless the parents get involved, their bullying child won't change. Unless you show why parents are connected to the bullying, then your solution — punishing parents — won't be very persuasive.

In our "No health care for obese people" topic you'd have to show that a financial penalty will help people lose weight.

> **MS. DUFFY'S TOP TIP**
> Real-life problems are caused by lots of things. You don't need to deny that a problem can have multiple causes to win a debate — you just need to say why your solution targets the most important cause.

4. Why This Will Solve It

You now need to explain why the change proposed by the topic will solve the problem. In most "should" debates, this is where the major disagreement happens: Is this solution going to work for this problem? It's your job to say "yes" or "no," depending on which side of the topic you're on, and explain why.

This is the hardest part of debating. You need to establish a cause/effect relationship between the problem and the solution that your team is proposing and then select the right tool for correcting what has been going wrong.

5. How? A Plan to Fix It

The first Proposition speaker has to present the plan. This is just a plan of what you'll do and how. It addresses the cause of the problem and says how to fix it.

A plan should take about twenty to thirty seconds to explain, and it should cover as many of the five Ws as you need: **who** will do **what**, **when**, and **where** and **why** it will work.

Your plan for our obesity topic might go like this:

- Health care will stop covering obesity-related illnesses in patients who are twenty percent or more over their ideal weight. They will be refunded if they lose weight. If their illness is due to other factors, they will not lose their health care.
- Two doctors will approve this for each patient.
- The scheme will start next year.
- After five years, there will be a review to see if the scheme has worked.

Then you explain why this plan solves the problem:

- It addresses the cause of the problem.
- It produces the right outcomes.

In another part of this book (starting on page 106) we go through a list of mechanisms that can be used to control, limit, or encourage certain actions, so that harms are kept to a minimum. The list includes banning, compelling, restricting, licensing, taxing, encouraging, and enforcing. Do any of these techniques suit the problem you are dealing with? If so, incorporate them into your plan.

Opposition

Responding to the Topic

The Opposition doesn't get to set the definition, but you should still be ready for what the Proposition is most likely to say. Ask the same questions they have so that you are prepared.

In some debating competitions it's okay to challenge the definition, but I recommend you just accept it. Otherwise it's hard to really get the debate to happen — you end up quibbling about the topic the whole time. True, sometimes a Proposition will give you a bad definition. Imagine they say "kids" in *Kids should have the right to vote* means "baby goats." This is very, very rare (and a stupid waste of time) and most students aren't that mean to their opponents. The adjudicator will be as outraged as you. Nobody who deliberately messes up a topic will win.

I once saw a debate where the team defined "grandparents" as "anyone over seventy." Is that what we mean by grandparents in everyday life? No. We mean people whose children have had children. This is not smart, it's silly.

Responding to the Problem

If you're the Opposition, you won't hear the case you are opposing until the debate is on. You have to prepare for what the Proposition is likely to say.

Your most important work is predicting what they'll say the problem is, why it matters, and how they'll fix it. You need to ask the same questions from the OPPOSITION point of view. Just imagine what you'd say if you were on the other side.

Three Ways to Disagree

Now that you've made a guess at what the Proposition will say the problem is, you have a strategic decision to make. The Opposition has three ways to disagree:

1. You can say, "No, there's no need to do anything. The problem's not as bad as you say, so just leave things alone."
2. You can say, "Yes, we agree there's a problem. Make the change but not in the way the Proposition wants. Here are some better ways."
3. You can say, "Yes, we agree there's a problem. But the Proposition's approach won't work and will actually make things worse."

If you don't agree that there is a problem, you can certainly say, "There's nothing wrong with the way

The Latin phrase for "the way things are" is **status quo**. Sometimes you'll hear people arguing for "maintaining the status quo." This is debaterspeak for "nothing needs to change."

the world is now, and there's no need to take action because there's nothing to solve! It doesn't matter that kids have bad handwriting." You're basically saying, "Meh — who cares?" Only do this when you're really sure there's nothing bad about what the Proposition is trying to fix.

Generally, you'll have a better case and a more fun debate by agreeing that there's a problem and having a disagreement about whether their plan will fix it.

Note that whichever way you choose, you're also going to want to think of reasons why their plan causes HARM as well as not solving the problem they want it to.

If you're agreeing there's a problem but saying that the Proposition's approach won't solve it, you need to say why not. The two ways to do this are the following:

1. **Look for causes and factors their plan doesn't touch.**

   For example, in our obesity example, what about all the causes of obesity that government health care won't be able to do anything about — for example, social pressure to eat badly, coming from a family where being fat is normal, being on a low income and buying cheap, fatty food because you have no choice, not caring what you weigh, cultural attitudes that say to be plump is good, and so on. You need to come up with a better way of helping these people to reach a healthy weight.

2. **Show that their solution will make things worse.**

   In this case the Opposition would say something like: "Obesity occurs more often when people have low incomes and low education. Making these people broke with new medical bills is going to add even more stress to an already difficult life. They will just decide not to go to the doctor, and this is going to make their health worse. Don't cut them off from the help they need."

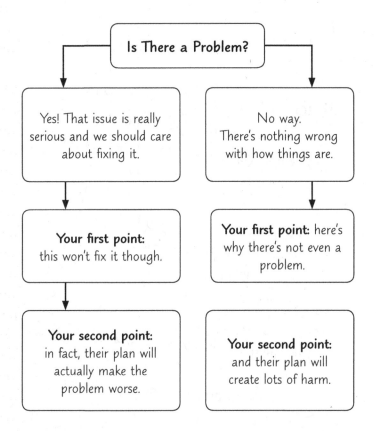

Is There a Problem?

Yes! That issue is really serious and we should care about fixing it.

No way. There's nothing wrong with how things are.

Your first point: this won't fix it though.

Your first point: here's why there's not even a problem.

Your second point: in fact, their plan will actually make the problem worse.

Your second point: and their plan will create lots of harm.

Opposition Case Plan

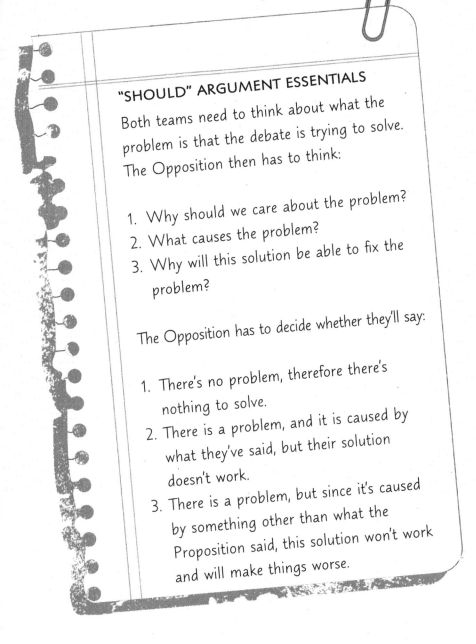

"SHOULD" ARGUMENT ESSENTIALS

Both teams need to think about what the problem is that the debate is trying to solve. The Opposition then has to think:

1. Why should we care about the problem?
2. What causes the problem?
3. Why will this solution be able to fix the problem?

The Opposition has to decide whether they'll say:

1. There's no problem, therefore there's nothing to solve.
2. There is a problem, and it is caused by what they've said, but their solution doesn't work.
3. There is a problem, but since it's caused by something other than what the Proposition said, this solution won't work and will make things worse.

How to Come Up With Points

Your next step is to think of precise points. But the good news is, you've already got some. Once you've thought about the problem for awhile, you should have at least your first point sorted out. It's this simple:

Point 1:
Why This Will/Will Not
Solve the Problem

There's a lot you can talk about here. It's usually a very big point and involves all the things we've covered so far. What's the problem? Who cares? What causes it? Does this fix it? Why/why not? It's very important that you set up all these issues carefully and clearly for your audience. You've spent all this time and energy coming up with answers to these questions, so make sure you remember to put them all in the first point.

Once that's done, you have a bit of free rein. Your other points are going to be about ways that the change proposed by the topic is good or bad.

Following are some points that usually appear later on in "should" debates.

Point 2:
It Is/Isn't Fair That We Do This

This means that there is some moral principle that is being violated. It's not right, or fair, or just. Does it go against some principle like freedom of speech or freedom of religion? Does it discriminate based on gender or age? You can make a whole point out of whether the solution is moral, quite aside from whether it will solve the problem you've already identified. For instance, if the topic was *We should lock up all criminals forever*, that would almost certainly solve the problem of a high crime rate, but would it be fair? No!

PRO TIP

Tell me why your solution connects to the problem — debates are always lost by people who didn't bother to explain in detail what the problem was, or who didn't show why their solution would solve it.
A senior adjudicator

Points 3 and 4:
The Effect on Stakeholders

This is a great way to target your arguments. Usually you can get one point per major stakeholder; for example, "This will be worse/better for parents because ..." or "This will be worse/better for the government because ..."

I like to think of stakeholders as being arranged on a line. Individuals are on the left, and at the far right we've got the whole world. All those stakeholders who could be affected by this debate topic lie somewhere in between:

- There are many different types of **individuals**: males, females, the young, the old, Indigenous peoples, the unemployed, wealthy people and poor people, people who belong to minority groups such as migrants or certain religions, and people who do or don't do something (go fishing, for example). Always consider specific types of individuals.
- **Families** are relevant because if one family member is affected by something, usually the whole family feels it in some way.

Stakeholders is debaterspeak for people affected by the issue being discussed.

- **Communities** are not just people who share a neighbourhood. There are other groups in all societies that form communities as well. A Vietnamese person could be part of the Vietnamese community, the wider migrant community, and their local business community. They might also be part of the birdwatching community, their children's school community, and the Buddhist community. Anyone reading this book is part of the debating community. What other communities do you belong to?

- **Institutions** are the organizations that make our society function. On home ground, the list includes the government (three levels: federal, state/provincial, and local), schools, hospitals, the courts, the police, the defence forces, religions, major businesses, banks, the stock market, major sporting associations, major political parties, and (very important!) the media.

- **The nation** is relevant if it's a topic that affects all of your country — and many do. There are also topics where the stakeholders are one or more of the states/provinces.

- You can go further, especially in some environmental or international debates, and include **international stakeholders** like the UN on issues which the whole world has an interest in.

You should work through this list — draw it on a whiteboard and tick off the stakeholders affected by the issue. Then decide which of them is the most important and consider what arguments would best relate to those stakeholders.

The stakeholder list above is just an example. You should adjust the stakeholders to suit your topic.

All done: a complete "should" case!

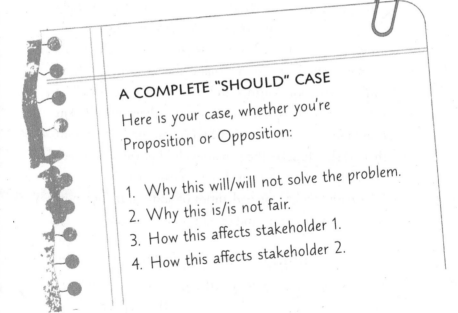

A COMPLETE "SHOULD" CASE

Here is your case, whether you're Proposition or Opposition:

1. Why this will/will not solve the problem.
2. Why this is/is not fair.
3. How this affects stakeholder 1.
4. How this affects stakeholder 2.

PREPARING "IS" TOPICS

"Is" topics, for example, *China is a bad influence*, don't call on you to make a change. They are a matter of judgement. They ask you to be convincing about how something is rather than argue that something should change. They say "Something-or-other does more harm than good," or "There is too much of something-or-other." ("Too much" means a damaging amount.)

Sometimes topics are metaphorical. They say something like "The carrot is better than the stick," or "The sun is rising once again." These are symbolic ideas, not really debates about carrots, sticks, or the fact that night is followed by day. You have to decide what real-life situations are represented by the carrot and the stick or the rising sun. Perhaps for "carrots and sticks" you could debate whether reward is more encouraging than punishment for school students and say (if you're on the Proposition) that we should relax the penalties children get when they misbehave. The sun rising could mean there has been a long dark "night," or bad times of some sort, but now things are looking up and good times are coming.

Defining an "Is" Topic

If you're proving that something's "good" or "better" you have to explain how you know. These are called criteria. You have to explain what standard you are judging by. What measures will you use?

You have to come up with a test — how do you know the thing is harmful/beneficial?

The Proposition will set the criteria because it's part of their definition. The Proposition needs to be neutral and use criteria that work for both sides. The Opposition has little choice but to accept the definition and criteria supplied by the Proposition.

You don't need a plan in an "is" debate, but you do need to answer similar questions to those in "should" debates. In fact, turning the "is" topic into a "should" topic can help you think it through. Let's say our topic is *Computer games do more harm than good.* Both sides of the debate might find it easier to prepare if they pretend the topic is *Computer games should be banned* and then brainstorm these three issues:

- Who is affected?
- How bad is it?
- What harm is it doing?

Decide on the Criteria

Whatever the statement is in the topic, ask yourself how you can judge whether this statement is true. By teasing out the reasons you "know" computer games are/are not harmful, you will get a sense of the criteria you can use. For example, on the Proposition:

- People are overweight — they relax with computer games instead of doing physical activity.
- Games isolate people from friends and family, leading to poor relationships, loneliness, and mental health problems.
- Violent games make violence seem normal — games could increase real-world violence.

So the Proposition could make the criteria about three types of wellbeing: physical, mental, and social.

Addressing the criteria the Proposition has chosen, the Opposition might argue:

- Games improve your spatial reasoning, reflexes, and memory. (Mental)
- Anything that exercises your brain is better than nothing! (Physical — sort of)
- Role playing the bad guy in a game helps you learn morals — how not to be a bad guy in real life. (Social)

The Opposition will have to accept the Proposition's criteria, so preparing the Opposition case means foreseeing what the Proposition is likely to come up with.

Consider the Stakeholders

The Proposition's job is to show that the criteria have been met, and the Opposition's is to show they haven't.

In "is" debates this is more often than not a game of

evidence: they bring an example, you say it doesn't matter; they bring an example, you say it isn't true. It's important to remember that you don't need to say that they're wrong or lying when they bring up a piece of evidence that seems to indicate one of their criteria has been fulfilled (or not) — you just need to show that what they're speaking about isn't representative: it's an outlier, just one example, and not representative of the whole truth.

If, for example, the topic was *Science has done more harm than good*, the Proposition might say, "It's thanks to science that we've had major medical malfunctions like Thalidomide." (A drug in the 1950s and 60s that caused birth defects in babies.) That's one very bad instance and not representative.

WHO SAYS WHAT: THE "ALLOCATION," "CASE DIVISION," OR "SPLIT"

Now you have an outline of what your case should look like if it's a "should" topic and what it should look like if it's an "is" topic. Time to split your points between your speakers and start writing them up in a way that will let you deliver your case to an audience.

The division of the points in your case is sometimes called the split or the allocation.

How should you divide your case up? It's a matter of personal preference, what suits the topic, and your approach to it.

The way you divide the points between the speakers in your team can be called the **allocation**, the **case division**, or the **split**.

You know how some people arrange their sock drawer according to colour — darks at the front, light at the back? And some arrange them by function — school socks separate from sport socks and dressy socks? Your debating case needs to be treated the same way. Organize your material according to the particular debate.

The general rule is that you should put the most important points first and the least important points last. If there's anything that jumps out at you as something you need to prove to win the debate, that should be in your first speaker's speech. If there was a point that you struggled to come up with, that should go in your second speaker's speech because it isn't the most important.

MS. DUFFY'S TOP TIP

Don't hoard points! Just because you thought of it doesn't mean you should be the one to say it.

NOW YOU KNOW In this section we have covered a lot of material. Case preparation has several steps and there are different processes depending on whether it's a "should" debate or an "is" debate.

- We've learned how to isolate the problem, explain the harm, locate the cause, and create a solution that will work.
- We've learned three ways to disagree if you are on the Opposition.
- We've looked at stakeholders and learned that you can frame your arguments around the people affected by the problem.
- We've seen that you have to split your case and share it among speakers so that the most important points are delivered by the first speakers.

Preparing a case well is the most important part of your debate. Use Ms. Duffy's (Complete) Debating Cheat Sheet (see page 268) to jog your memory and make sure you don't leave anything out.

GIVE IT A GO!

Working With Definitions

Here are some topics at different levels of difficulty. See if you can work out how to treat them. Work out if they're "should" or "is" topics. Interpret any tricky phrases. Come up with a definition that is reasonable and fair.

- *We should stop the government funding of zoos.*
- *Sporting teams should be selected according to merit, not gender.*
- *Every student should learn a second language.*
- *It is unfair to tell children there's a Santa Claus.*
- *More people should walk to work.*
- *The school day should last longer.*
- *Schools should put students under video surveillance.*

Practise With the Problem

Let's say our topic is *Helmets should be compulsory for cyclists*, and we're on the Proposition. Let's work through the most important part of the debate: the problem.

Step one: What is the problem that this topic is trying to solve?

That's right, head injuries to people who ride bikes.

Step two: Why should we care?

I guess the answer is obvious. Brain damage is on most people's list of "things I don't want to have." It also hurts the people around the injured person and costs a great deal of money in medical care.

Step three: What causes the problem?

Again, pretty obvious: A rider's head whacks the ground when they fall or get knocked off. Cyclists are unprotected, exposed, and vulnerable. It's just the way cycling is.

Step four: Why will the solution given to you in the topic — making helmets compulsory — solve the problem?

Answer — once again, pretty obvious: it shields and protects the skull.

Let's switch to the Opposition. Do you agree that there is a problem?

Given the severity of brain injuries it's probably sensible to say "yes," there is a problem, and to agree that we should care about it. So now you have to say that while there's a problem, the solution proposed by the Proposition (helmets) won't work. Remember there were two ways to do that:

1. Because the problem is caused by something that their solution won't target.
2. Because their solution won't have any effect on what they say is the cause of the problem.

Try each one of them in turn:

1. Bike accidents are caused by a whole lot of things:
    car drivers, traffic, and road and weather conditions,
    for a start. We need accident *prevention*, not just
    protection. To really keep cyclists safe we need
    everyone to be more bike aware so accidents don't
    happen in the first place. Bike lanes, high visibility
    clothing, and rules to keep cars at a distance will
    do more good than helmets.
2. Helmets are not effective.

In this example you'd best choose Number 1, as
it's hard to accept that a helmet wouldn't protect a
cyclist's head.

Your final job on the Opposition is to show that
their solution actually makes things worse.

Brainstorm a list of ways this model might happen.

Here's one answer: "Helmets produce a false sense
of security. Riders and drivers both see that cyclists are
protected. They forget how vulnerable they really are and
don't take proper care. Not only does this solution not fix
the problem of head injuries, it actually makes it worse!"

Who Are the Stakeholders?

The following are three different examples. Which group of
stakeholders is most important to each debate? Develop
some headline points that you could use in your case.

- If the debate is about cyber bullying at school, the "individuals" stakeholder category would mean the **victims** and the **bullies**. "Family" and "community" stakeholders would be **friends** and **families** of both victims and bullies. "Institutions" include their teachers, their **schools**, the **principal** and other staff, and the **police**. Perhaps the media the bully uses (for example, Facebook) is also a stakeholder. The debate could possibly say this is a nationwide problem and include **the country** in the stakeholders but should probably not include "the world."
- If the topic is about recycling, you might say the stakeholders are **households** and **families**, institutions like **schools** and **shops** (which use recycling), the recycling **industry**, and (eventually) the **planet**.
- In a topic about limiting visitors to the Grand Canyon, you would have stakeholders from nearly every category. The **planet** is affected by environmental damage as plant and animal species die out and water sources are threatened; the American **government** has **international** responsibilities because of the canyon's global importance as an ecological wonder; in **Arizona**, lots of people depend on tourism to the Grand Canyon, and the state economy needs the income; there are many **institutions** involved in protecting the site and running the park and the tourist

93

areas; and of course there are the many **families** and **individuals** who visit, work in the tourism industry, or live nearby.

Find the Cause

Think through these cases in more detail, filling in any missing information first. Then come up with a first Proposition speech outline that explains the cause of the problem in terms that connect it tightly to the topic, making the topic a good solution. Remember to give plenty of examples and evidence!

Solution (Topic)	Problem?	Harm?	Cause?
The school day should start later.	Tiredness — kids are unproductive, inattentive. Roads are clogged with peak-hour traffic.	Bad for education, student focus, family stability. Getting to school and work is slow and stressful.	Teen sleep cycles are different, they naturally sleep late. Schools and businesses everywhere start and finish at nearly the same time.
Parents should have access to their children's social media accounts.	Children at risk from inappropriate friendships — parents can't help/protect.	Children get into trouble — get hurt or damaged. Can be very serious.	
Computer games are bad.	Children so engrossed with games that they miss out on other life experiences.		
We should change the flag.			

4

Rights Debates

Often you'll get "should" debates that are about rights. Any debate topic that says we should ban, restrict, encourage, or enforce something is a "rights debate." That's because it wants you to change someone's right to do something-or-other. The reason behind this is that when they exercise that right, it does some harm, to them or someone else.

Most school debates with the word "should" in them are about finding the balance between rights and harms. They are so common that this whole chapter is about "rights versus harms" debates so that you can learn a basic approach to preparing them.

WHAT ARE RIGHTS?

Rights and freedoms work in two ways:

1. You have the right/are free to do things: speak your mind, believe in any religion you like, control what happens to your own body.

2. You have the right to be free from some things: violence, harassment, or discrimination.

But what are rights? Where do they come from? This is a complicated question. It causes disagreements between very brainy people in several different fields of study. We are not going to join in this discussion; we're going to learn only what you need to know to win a debate, and it's this MOST IMPORTANT FACT: "Should ..." is not the same as "should be allowed to ..."

Saying somebody should be allowed to do something is saying they have a right to it, whether or not it's good for them (or for society). For instance, adults have a right to control their own bodies (it's known in debating as "bodily autonomy"). This means they can drink alcohol and eat a kilo of chocolate every night if they want to. Should they? Probably not. Should they be allowed to? Yes!

WHO HAS RIGHTS?

In a democratic society like ours, adults have rights. If a person isn't physically or mentally able to exercise those rights (maybe they are in a coma or have a medical condition that prevents them), someone else gets the power to act on their behalf. A family member or a person appointed by the government will do this for them.

Rights are a big deal in the United States. Often on American TV shows you'll see people talk about "the right to remain silent" or their "right to an attorney." Other countries are different and don't have such a protected and publicly known list of rights. Be careful that you don't name American rights by accident in a non-American debate! I once saw a debater talk about "taking the fifth." Uh-oh — there is no "fifth" outside the U.S.

Rights of Children and Responsibilities of Parents

The biggest group of people with limited rights in our society is children and young people. It is not until you are an adult that your full rights come your way.

Why is this? It's because children and young people can't be depended upon to make mature, sensible decisions. It's not your fault — your brains are not developed fully. You have poor impulse control, not much life experience, and your values are not yet in good shape. But you'll grow out of it.

For the same reasons, our society says that even criminal offences by a young person are not the same as those by an adult. Children have their own courts, they don't go to adult jails, and the names of child criminals are not published. A child will be treated more favourably than an adult who committed the same crime.

While children are growing, we expect parents and schools to take on a "duty of care" and keep them from harm till they can be responsible for themselves. This is often at the heart of a debate topic. There are lots of arguments about

- whether children deserve this "different" treatment;
- how much blame and responsibility parents and schools can reasonably accept, and how much the child is responsible; and
- whether the current age limits are the right ones.

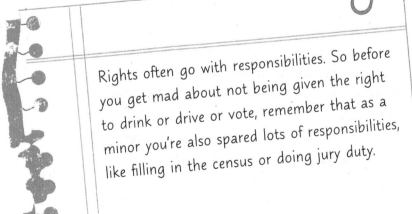

Rights often go with responsibilities. So before you get mad about not being given the right to drink or drive or vote, remember that as a minor you're also spared lots of responsibilities, like filling in the census or doing jury duty.

The Role of Government

A democratic government is expected to take care of its citizens. The idea is that because we all participate in choosing the government, it will look after us.

So the government sets the rules that allow us to exercise our rights. This can test another important democratic principle, which is that we "live and let live." People are free to do pretty well anything in a democracy like ours, unless it harms or endangers another person. If there's a harm or danger, the government steps in to stop it by making laws.

It sounds simple, but in real life we don't agree on what "harm" or "danger" are; and we disagree about whose rights and freedoms matter most or what the best sorts of limits are.

Think about the case on page 46 when you wanted to go and watch a friend's game on a school night. Is Mom limiting your rights fairly when she says "No"? Has she stepped in to prevent harm, or is she just being mean?

Suppose you want to ban off-leash dogs from the park near your house. They bug you when you're playing ball games, they poo and their owners don't clean up, and they're potentially dangerous, you say. "We want a safe and clean park!" you cry. Dog owners reply that you already have one. Only dogs under owners' control are allowed off the leash. These dogs are not a danger, they say, and owners *do* clean up. "We want to exercise our pets!" they say. It seems that both sides have merit. How is the local council going to decide?

Rights and Community Standards

It's easy to see that a government should protect its citizens in a physical sense, but government also has to protect us from things that hurt us in other ways — things that disturb us, cause offence, invade our privacy, or upset or inconvenience us. The government has a whole lot of laws and rules that support current community values. These make it easier for our whole society to live together and function properly.

For example, the government supports individuals' right to control their own lives, and says that things can't be done to us without our knowledge and permission. Patients must consent to treatment — a surgeon can't remove or replace a part of you unless you've agreed. You can't eavesdrop, or access a person's phone records, or enter their property without their permission. You can't harass someone or say damaging things about them.

There are also rules about what's decent and respectable. We don't allow people to wander the streets naked (even in hot weather!). Men can't use women's public restrooms and vice versa. We don't allow drunk and disorderly behaviour in public, and there's even a point where we don't allow it in private — that's why "concerned neighbours" get the police to come and quiet down a wild party.

WHERE TO DRAW THE LINE?
WHAT LINE TO DRAW?

What is accepted as "normal" and "acceptable" varies. How we like to live changes over time and differs from place to place, and there are lots of vigorous debates in the real world about changing the way some matters are managed. In a debate you will be able to argue for change more easily if you know that your country's way of doing things is not the only way things can be done.

For instance:

- The age at which you can drive, leave school, get married, or be charged with a crime as an adult varies widely around the world.
- In some places you can buy alcohol in the same shops you buy groceries. In other places, alcohol sales and consumption are very tightly controlled.
- Face coverings, including the burqua, are banned in public in some countries. In others, it's compulsory for women to be covered.
- In many parts of the U.S. you can join the army and fight for your country before you are old enough to go into a bar.
- In some countries mothers leave their babies in strollers outside the store while they do their shopping. In other countries that would be considered child neglect.

- Many countries allow pets on public transportation and in shops and restaurants.

Deciding when to impose controls and limits and what type of controls and limits to use is the debater's big challenge.

RIGHTS AND HARMS IN THE BALANCE

Debates about rights say that the rights and freedoms of some people should be changed: they should have more or less of a right to do something.

Imagine that rights and harms are sitting on opposite ends of a see-saw. In a debate, if we put maximum restrictions on rights and freedoms, the "rights" side of the see-saw will go up, and the "harms" end will go down — there will be few or no harms. For example, restricting people's right to smoke helps avoid the harm of cancer.

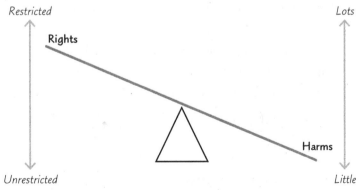

Rights and Harms in the Balance

An easy mistake to make is to play loosey-goosey with the term "right." I've seen debaters say schoolchildren have a "right to lunchtime," and that adults have a "right to connect with each other on social media." Really? What international agreement lists "lunch" and "Facebook"? When in doubt, just say "people should be allowed to" instead of "have a right to."

If the debate says to loosen up and give people unrestricted rights, the rights end of the see-saw will go down, and the harms end will rise — that is, the harms would be greater. If we let people smoke, the amount of cancer will increase.

HANDLING RIGHTS AND HARMS DEBATES

To argue these cases, in the debate you must

- think about the rights and harms in question and name them;
- say why they matter to this debate; and

- say why the rights should be upheld or the harms should be limited.

A good way of persuading your audience that certain rights matter is to use a comparison — name a similar situation where this right is taken very seriously. For example, a parent should be allowed to prevent their child from getting body piercings, because it's important that a parent takes care of their child's body, which is accepted — parents can already permit or prevent their child from having procedures in hospital.

In the topic *Helmets should be compulsory for cyclists* the Opposition will say cyclists have a right to make their own decisions about what risks their bodies are exposed to. But the Proposition will say that the risk of harm is too great; that these riders' rights should be quashed to protect the bike riders, their families, and the health-care system from the consequences of a terrible accident.

The Proposition could

- **name the right**: There is nothing more important than the safety of human life.
- **say why it should be upheld**: Losing even one cyclist needlessly to brain damage is too big a price to pay.
- **offer a comparison**: We make seatbelts compulsory for exactly the same reasons.

- **explain why it's worth doing despite opposition**: The inconvenience and costs are small in comparison to the benefit. We are saving brains, helping to keep people alive. The bike riders who don't like it at first will get used to it. Everyone will be happier to "cycle in safety."

See if you can work out what the Opposition team's view would be.

THE TOOLKIT FOR CHANGE

If your team is going to make a change to something, you need to say how. This is part of developing a case for a "should" topic, detailed on pages 63–83.

You have a range of options. Put simply, you have to decide whether to use "carrots" to motivate and inspire the desired behaviour; or "sticks" to deter and punish the bad behaviour. Then you must choose which specific carrot or stick will best do the job.

Sanctions and Penalties

You also need to decide how you will enforce the rules. If you can't, then you are on weak ground. What sort of trouble will follow if people don't stay within these new limits? There must be consequences, a penalty.

Generally speaking, a punishment should fit a crime. We expect to see severe penalties (like jail or very heavy fines) for people who do something serious — break a ban or don't do something that's compulsory. Milder punishments are given for lesser offences.

You probably can already see how much debate could go on about whether penalties are tough enough for any particular offence.

Controls and Limits

Opposite is a table that shows the different ways we deter undesirable behaviour and encourage desirable behaviour. In the next section we'll look at them in some detail.

Banning/Compelling

These are the heavyweights of controls and limits. We ban someone from doing something and compel someone to do something. You ban something because it is really harmful. You compel something because it is really good.

For example:

- Certain drugs are banned. You are not allowed to use them. They are dangerous because they are addictive and harmful. People get hurt. Badly hurt. Penalties are very heavy to turn people off offending in the first place.
- "Total fire bans" can come into effect during forest fire season. Fire damage is catastrophic. It must be

Rights Debates

The Government Says	How It's Controlled	Penalties	Examples
STOP! Don't ever do this. It's BAD for you and for our society.	It's completely BANNED.	Jail and heavy fines.	Illegal drug Slavery Cigarette advertising Underage sex
This is okay for SOME people to do in SOME circumstances. We want to limit the chance of harm.	We issue LICENCES, make RULES and REGULATIONS, and set STANDARDS.	You will be stopped and fined.	Doctors, pharmacies, lawyers, taxis, pubs and clubs, marriage celebrants, broadcasters, builders, banks, waste disposal ... and many more.
We'd RATHER you DIDN'T do this too much, so we're making it · HARD.	We TAX, LIMIT, or RESTRICT the activity.	Fines	Buying and drinking alcohol Playing loud music Causing pollution
We WANT you to do this, because it's GOOD for you and the rest of us.	We promote, advertise, educate, inform, reward, subsidise, or provide the service.	You miss out on the benefits.	Drive safely Be vaccinated in childhood Don't drink too much Exercise regularly and eat well
We INSIST you do this because it's good for you and the rest of us.	It's ENFORCED. We COMPEL you.	Jail and heavy fines.	Wear seatbelts Go to school Drive on the right Wear clothes

avoided. A total ban prevents accidents. The penalties are jail or a fine of several thousand dollars.

- Smoking is banned in many public places because it is so harmful to the health not only of the smokers, but also of the people around them. Heavy fines apply.

In these cases, the government overrides an individual's right to take drugs, have a campfire in a heatwave, or choose to smoke, because in our community we say "No" — you don't get to endanger yourself or anyone else by doing those things.

At the positive end, we compel people to do certain things because they make us all safer or help our society run well, and we are all better off. For example:

- We all must go to school.
- Everyone in a car must wear a seatbelt.
- All drivers must drive on the right and follow the road rules.
- All income earners must pay tax.

When everybody does these things, the whole community functions better. These arrangements work because the whole population has to comply.

Restricting, Limiting, Licensing, Regulating

We allow some things at certain times or in certain places or circumstances:

- There are age limits: on voting, drinking, getting married, seeing some movies.
- We limit land use: you can't build a factory on a residential street; some important old buildings cannot be demolished; national parks can only be used for certain types of activities.
- We have time restrictions: bars and pubs have limited hours; you cannot make excessive noise at night; airplanes cannot fly during certain hours at night; truck drivers must take regular rest breaks.
- We regulate or license things: you can't drive without a licence; medicine can only be obtained from qualified and registered doctors and pharmacists; banks, schools, hospitals, law firms, and insurance companies are just some of the businesses that have to meet a lot of standards before the government will let them operate.

Ask around and you will find lots of people you know have had to go through some sort of formal process to be allowed to do their job.

Taxes

A tax is when the government takes a share of what you earn or a slice of the price of something. Tax is how the government collects the money it needs to run the country. We have to have it. The quarrel is always about how much tax and on what.

One way to deter some behaviour is to make it very expensive. If affordability is important to people, the idea is that if you make the thing cost more, fewer people will buy it. You can price the harmful thing out of reach.

For instance, if you want people to buy locally made goods, tax similar goods that are imported from other countries. Luxury items like French perfume are more expensive than the local version.

If you want people to stop smoking and drinking, put the price of cigarettes and alcohol way up. By the same logic, if you want to stop obesity, you could make sweets or junk food really expensive as well.

Don't be fooled by the simple logic of all this. For example, if you did tax fast food that would not please the fast food chains, who will lose customers and then income, and that will mean there aren't many jobs for young people flipping burgers, so youth unemployment will rise.... You may have created a fresh problem!

Encouragement, Education, Incentives, and Services

Instead of putting up barriers, we can sweeten people up and help them to do the "good" things by making them easy and attractive.

Public **education and advertising** campaigns make doing the right thing popular. Think about ads for road safety, sun safety, being active, and safe alcohol consumption. Make the desired behaviour cool and it is more likely to happen.

Sometimes the government uses the direct **financial appeal**. They give cash for recycling or a reward for informing to the police. There are tax refunds if you give money to charities or take steps to "green" your home. Some industries that the government wants to develop have tax incentives to encourage investment.

Sometimes the government steps in and **"just does it."** Take immunizations for children at school. What could be simpler? Some governments provide the service for free. Parents are happy because their children are protected. They don't even need a trip to the clinic, because the clinic comes to the school. The whole population benefits because dangerous illnesses are suppressed.

There are many real life debates between people who think the government should be making rules and regulations for us and those who think that the government should stay out of our lives. If the government is seen to be overly involved in people's daily lives, this is called "the nanny state." The idea is that the government is treating its citizens like little children who cannot take care of themselves.

Ask around at home and see what your family thinks.

"The Black Market" Argument

When a topic says something should be banned, the Opposition response might be that if it's popular and people want it, they will find a way around the ban. It will continue but in secret, illegally. There will be what's called a "black market."

The best known example of this is when alcohol was banned in the United States in the 1920s. The illegal trade in alcohol that followed brought lawlessness, corruption, and violence. It did a lot of harm — perhaps more than the alcohol would have done.

During the Second World War, supplies of the most basic items were rationed. They were very scarce and legally restricted. There was a black market in everything from food and drink to clothing and gasoline. People traded illegally if they could get hold of goods outside the official channels.

Current examples of the black market include illegal migrant workers; pirated music and movies; counterfeit designer clothes; guns; illegal animal products such as whale meat, ivory, and rhino horn; and, of course, illegal drugs, including those used in sports.

The argument against a ban is that if there's a black market, the thing we are trying to stop doesn't go away — it's still happening, only now it's unregulated and open to abuse. It's better to control the unwanted thing with laws and rules than to impose a ban that will start an illegal market, which in turn leads to more harm.

 NOW YOU KNOW Many school debates involve balancing rights and harms. When your debate asks you to change what someone is allowed to do, you need to explain why that will bring a benefit and prevent a harm. You also have to choose the best technique for making the change, and you need to think of some consequences or penalties that fit the situation, which will ensure your change will work.

If you're on the Opposition team and your opponents want to put a stop to something that is popular, defend your position by saying that this will just send it underground and create a black market.

GIVE IT A GO! Talking about debatable issues with your friends and family is a great way to see a subject from a number of different angles. If it gets heated, please don't throw things. Debating is a *verbal* skill. Explain why you think what you do. Practise expressing the harms and the benefits of the issues.

The examples below turn up in school debates all the time. It would be a good idea to have discussed them in advance. Remember there's no right and wrong: they genuinely have two (or more) sides. The issues in conflict are in bold, to steer your discussion in the right direction, but you may come up with others.

Discussion 1

The right to control your own body ("bodily autonomy")
Responsibility to care for children and young people
There are many debates about parents' rights and responsibilities in their children's lives. At what age can a child have an independent opinion? Should the child's wishes be taken into account for some important life decisions? Should a child accept their parents' decisions? Do children prefer their parents to make the decisions? Until what age should a young person do what their parent decides?

For example: should a parent get cosmetic surgery for their child? If the parent and child don't agree, who gets to decide? Does it make a difference what the surgery is for? What about the permanence of the result? How do you feel about a parent arranging surgery for big ears, birthmarks, moles, or nose jobs? Do you feel the same way about body piercing and tattoos? What if the aim is to win a modelling contract or an acting role? Does the age of the child make a difference?

Try talking over the right to privacy (both online and in other ways); the right to choose a school and what subjects to study; to choose your own friends; or to decide which parent you will live with after a divorce. Do you and your parents see things the same way?

Discussion 2

Public figures as role models
Public figures' right to privacy

It's often said that we live in a celebrity culture. Should people who are "stars" in public life also excel at the ordinary, private side of life? Why? Does their personal life affect their professional performance? What if their private life *is* their professional life (think about the Kardashians).

When a pop singer has a drug problem (this happens often), does the public need to know? Why? What if it's in the past and they're off drugs now and clean? How about a sports star with a mental health problem? If a politician got stage fright, would we want it publicized? What if they stole something? How about a famous person with a child who is in trouble with the law?

Does it change the person's right to privacy if they didn't cause the issue — for example, if it was an accident or a medical or family problem outside their control?

In all these cases, what difference does it make if the public knows or does not know?

What does the media get from publicizing personal stories like these? What about the public figures? Don't celebrities *want* publicity? How would they be famous otherwise?

Discussion 3

The individual right to privacy
The right to live in a secure society

Some people say "Privacy — get over it!" What does this mean? Do you agree? Should we be under surveillance? Is it alright to be watched without knowing about it? What about when shops and banks collect information about us based on what we buy and how we spend our money? Is there a difference between being watched by part of the government (for example the police, Customs, or the security service) rather than by a commercial organization like a private investigator, shop, or insurance company? What should they be able to do with this information? Can I be sure they won't use the information unfairly? What could I do if I did not trust them?

Is it reasonable to put certain racial or religious groups under closer scrutiny, on the basis that risk of harm from these groups is greater than from other parts of the community? (This is called "profiling.")

Discussion 4

The right to "free assembly" (that is, to get together whenever and wherever you like)
The right to public safety
Should music festivals be banned, given the known dangers of dealing with crowd control and the likelihood of alcohol and drug abuse? What about organized political rallies, demonstrations, and protest marches, which sometimes become angry and violent? What effect would it have if these events were not allowed? Who would suffer and how?

Discussion 5

The right to seek asylum
The right to control our country's borders
Should our country take in more of the world's refugees? If not, where should they go? What reason is there to put asylum seekers in detention?

What reasons are there not to? Why do you think this issue causes such heated debate?

Discussion 6

The right to free speech
The right to religious freedom
If someone does not respect another's religion, can they say so? If so, how should the person being criticized respond? What is "hate speech"? How is it different from "free speech"? Is it still "free speech" to say certain things when there's a payoff — publicity, for example? Is it better to cause offence by speaking up or avoid upsetting others by keeping quiet? In what circumstances do we accept that lying is acceptable?

5

The Point — The Building Block of Debates

You know now that a case is made up of points, but how *exactly* do you make a point? What has to come out of your mouth? If you learn nothing else from this book, make sure this section is the ONE thing that sticks in your mind.

A **point** is the basic unit in a debate. You need to make strong points and link them together to make a solid case. If debating were Lego, a point would be a single brick. Linked up together, the bricks make a strong wall of argument.

A **point** is the basic unit in a debate. You need to make strong points and link them together to make a solid case.

THE PREP APPROACH

A well-made point is clear, direct, and relevant. It has four parts. The four-part formula is the most important of all debating techniques. It's called **PREP**, and we're going to learn to use it now. Here's how it goes.

PREP stands for Point Reason Example Proved. Commit it to memory and say it as you drop off to sleep at night and when you wake up again in the morning. Say it as you jog around the track, clean your teeth, or practise your scales. It's your friend for life.

P: A **point** starts with a simple statement of one slice of your argument.

In debaterspeak this is called an **assertion**. By itself, it is not enough. In fact, an assertion just dropped out there, all bald and unclothed, is a bad thing in debating, and you'll be criticized for it.

R: Expand on it and back it up with **reasons**.

Reasons explain. They show cause and effect. They open your point up and expose it to inspection and analysis. By exploring, elaborating, and adding depth and weight to the discussion, reasons and explanations build believability. Have you ever heard someone say, "I'm entitled to my opinion"? Well yes, they are. But they are not entitled to expect others to listen to it, unless there are good reasons to do so.

Debaters need to practise explaining and giving reasons for their opinions. No matter how complex the issue, the foundation of debating is to be able to give good reasons. Finding good reasons means asking yourself over and over, "Why?" and saying "This matters because …"

The very best reasons are tangible. That means "able to be touched," easily recognized, clear, and definite. If whatever you're saying is real, observable, actual, seeable, and feelable, it is more convincing.

E: Now you must introduce some supporting **examples**.

Find real evidence that fits the point you're making. That word "evidence" is important. Evidence includes examples and stories from real life. These are the things that move your argument out of the realm of imagination and into reality: believable, true, and trustworthy. Phrases like "It is generally agreed that …" and "In our society, we expect people to …" or "It's normal to punish/not allow/discourage …" can help you out here.

P: Why this **proves** your case — why the point matters overall.

Return to your initial point and remind the audience why it's important for your case. Summarize what you've said in one sentence and use the phrase "This matters because …" When you conclude this way, it will click into place in the adjudicator's mind as a well-made point that has been proved.

Sample PREP in Action

Let's say our topic is *We should ban alcohol advertising in sports.*

Point: Advertising alcohol in sports links a healthy, hugely popular activity with an unhealthy and damaging one. It's unethical, misleading, and puts public health at risk.

Reason/Explanation: Alcohol is a dangerous drug that causes major health and social problems. In ads at sporting events it's disguised as a normal part of having a good time. The ads create a false impression. Drinking beer does not make you run fast and score goals — it's more likely to make you fall down and vomit.

Example: We know that smoking is bad, and some countries have banned cigarette ads altogether. It's time to treat alcohol the same way.

Proved: Advertising at sporting events misleads people about the dangers of alcohol, and this is just one of the reasons why it should be banned.

Debates are won by making good points. Points have four parts. You need reasons to **explain** and **justify** your point, and you need **examples** and **evidence** to back up what you are saying.

MS. DUFFY'S TOP TIP

If your point is mainly about the rights and wrongs or morality of an issue ("It's just not right!"), it could be hard to come up with real-life examples to support it. Think about how we know something is not right. Perhaps it's usually not allowed, or is usually punished, or there's a law or a rule or agreement somewhere saying how this situation should work out. So focus on the principles involved.

WHAT NOT TO DO

Here are some techniques to avoid.

Don't Make Stuff Up

You sound silly if you say things like "Dr. Madeupname from the Definitely Real University conducted a study in which 99 per cent of respondents proved our case." Well, they didn't. You know that, the adjudicator knows that, and your opponent knows that, too. It's not persuading anyone and it wastes time.

Avoid "Imaginaries"

If you say "How would you like it if ..." or "Imagine Jessica was walking home one day when ..." you are not on strong ground. The whole purpose of examples is to provide real proof. If you can only think of imaginary examples, you should reconsider whether your point is a good one.

Don't Assume the Audience Is the Same as You

You will debate people from varied backgrounds. They all have different opinions, beliefs, politics, and religions, and they will have very different life experiences from your own. Make sure your evidence and the examples you use will make sense beyond your own social group. Explain the examples you are using so that a person who is unfamiliar with them will still get your point.

Don't Tell Your Own Story

Personal experiences don't belong in a debate and should only be used if they point to a general truth about the issue more widely — which is unlikely. Personal stories are easy to rebut, because they are too specific. You also risk causing embarrassment, as you may say things in public that would be better left private.

Don't Use Manipulative Language

There is a fine line between persuasive and manipulative language. Manipulative language is unreasonable. It twists the information. It doesn't allow opposition. It closes the door on debate.

Some debaters appeal to highly emotional values like fairness, patriotism, safety, trust, honour, or respect. These are loose general terms but loaded with the idea that they are good. They may or may not be justified, but because they wear the halo of goodness it can be daunting to attack them. You can feel like you are doing something you shouldn't.

Also, although we've said that debates are won by logic and reason, some debate topics themselves can arouse strong emotions. Think of how worked up people get about animal cruelty, refugees, environmental issues, or national security. These issues can be hard to argue, because strong feelings cloud your thinking.

Listen to what they say, ignore the way they say it. Keep a cool head. In a school debate you don't have to mean what you say.

A POORLY MADE POINT ...

- presents no convincing proof
- uses no information that could be checked
- makes generalizations, with no specific cases
- uses emotional language, while glossing over the facts.

If a debater is getting heated and using a lot of emotional statements with not too many examples, it could be a sign that their reasoning is faulty — or missing altogether. So listen to what they say and ignore the way they say it.

NOW YOU KNOW Debates are won by making good points. Points have four parts. You need to

1. State the point (also called an assertion).
2. Give reasons to explain and justify it.
3. Provide real-world examples and evidence to back up what you're saying.
4. Say exactly what you have proved just in case the adjudicator missed it.

6

Really Good Rebuttal

Rebuttal is the heart and soul of debating. To win a debate you can't just come up with better arguments than the other team — you have to find fault with your opposition directly and actively, completely tear them DOWN. Put on your boxing gloves. You need to hit hard at whatever they say. No lily-livered weaklings here, please — this is the time to be tough.

All debates are about proving the other side is mistaken, incorrect, unconvincing. To do this you must address "the clash," the big point of conflict, as well as attack the weak spots in every point they make.

Rebuttal occupies about half of a team's case, and the further into the debate you speak, the more rebuttal you must present. It's like defensive play on the sports field. You have to be out there stopping the other team from scoring.

REBUTTAL BASICS

When you rebut, you must find faults in the other team's reasoning and attack their arguments. You need to be on the hunt for any weakness.

Three Things to Target

You've already learned about PREP and how to make a four-part point. When you are rebutting your opposition, look at their four-part-points to discover where they are weakest. Then take aim and fire!

You can target your rebuttal at

- **P:** the main idea, their top level **point.** This is the strongest form of rebuttal. You can knock a point out on moral and/or practical grounds. Show that it
  - is unfair or unprincipled, the wrong thing to do;
  - won't work, won't solve the problem;
  - leads to the wrong result; or
  - is not addressing the main problem.
- **R:** their **reasoning**, explanations, and analysis. Show that they are illogical and don't make sense. This is a very powerful way to rebut. Check the section on fallacies (see pages 32–44) to get this one right.
- **E:** their **examples** or evidence. Show that these are incorrect, or misleading, because they really

tell a different story. This is not usually a strong form of rebuttal, because a poor example does not automatically mean it's a poor point. By all means correct a weak example, but say why it makes the *argument* weak as well.

Watch also for inconsistencies and contradictions between speakers. If one of them said something was affordable and another said it costs a lot but it's money well spent, perhaps they are not clear about their case.

How to Attack

Rebuttals also have four parts, so you can use our old friend **PREP**. You just

1. state the **point** you believe is wrong;
2. explain the **reasons** you think it's wrong;
3. give **examples**; and
4. conclude by saying what this **proves**.

You will use the words "because" and "therefore" to make your rebuttal complete, just as you do when you make your own points.

A basic way to rebut goes like this:

"They say ..." (summarize briefly what they did say, in ten words or less).

"But we say ..." (give your alternative view of the issue).

"Because …" (explain the reasons they are at fault and why their argument is no good. In a second sentence give an example to support it).

"Therefore …" (why you are convincing and they are not).

For example: "**They say** that we should limit the number of people going to the Grand Canyon in order to slow down its destruction, but **we say** it's important to allow as many people as possible to see the canyon, **because** keeping people away means the damage is "out of sight, out of mind," and the public will not get to know how bad the situation is. For **example**, by encouraging tourists to go to the Galapagos Islands to see the giant tortoises, their government helped spread the word about the species that live there and the importance of saving their habitat. Tourism created awareness and motivated people from all over the world to help. The funds raised from tourism are saving those species from extinction. **Therefore**, tourism can be good for the environment, and we should promote tourism to the Grand Canyon."

MS. DUFFY'S TOP TIP
Rebuttal makes up about a third to a half of your speech if you are First Opposition or a second speaker. It takes nearly all your speech if you are Second Opposition.

THEMATIC REBUTTAL

Basic rebuttal like the example above treats the opposition's points as if they were tennis balls to be returned one at a time. They make a point (*pok!*), so you rebut it (*pok!*). When you are starting out as a debater, that is exactly what you should do.

The trouble is that picking on every little tiny bad example or illogical thing they've said gets repetitive and begins to sound like a shopping list or a tennis game that will never end (*pok pok pok pok pok pok pok pok pok* ... yawn). It's good to show the adjudicator that you've picked up problems with every point they've made, but it's better to lift rebuttals to a higher level and tell a story about why the whole case is unconvincing.

Think of it this way: why chop a tree down branch by branch when a blow to the trunk will remove it whole?

If you are a second speaker (there's not enough material available for firsts to use this approach), try to group your rebuttals into "families" or themes. The skill is to identify the big ideas that sit like an umbrella, covering a number of their points, and then deal with all the points in that whole bundle, instead of just in the order they presented them. This is known as thematic rebuttal.

Thematic rebuttal is when you identify the larger ideas that cover a number of your opposition's points and deal with them as a bundle, rather than in the order they presented them.

FINDING THE FLAWS IN THE OTHER TEAM'S ARGUMENTS

We already know that good arguments are clear, accurate, precise, relevant, broad, deep, and logical. As you listen, ask yourself: how well do the other side's arguments fit this description? Does what they say make sense? Is their evidence reliable? Does it fit the topic? Have they given you speculation and opinion not supported by facts? If you are familiar with the common fallacies, it will also help you spot the problems that exist in their case.

The Faulty Four

Here is a list of common flaws in school debates — I call it the Faulty Four. It is not a complete list, but it shows the typical errors student debaters make.

All four ways to be wrong are closely related, and the borders between them are easily crossed, so the list is not perfect. Still, you should memorize it, as it will help you decide where to aim your rebuttals.

1. Not in the real world! They are suggesting that things work in a way they do not.
   - Their facts are wrong.
   - They lack evidence; for example, they are using unsupported assertions, opinions, or speculation.
   - Their examples are misleading.
2. Their moral position is flawed. What they want to do is unprincipled — just not right.
   - It causes harm.
   - It's unfair or degrading.
   - It limits someone's freedom without good reason.
3. Their logic is flawed.
   - They're misleading or distorting.
   - They're telling only part of the story.
   - They're generalizing when it's not justified.
4. Their points are irrelevant. They do not address the main issue.

The meatiest of these is Type 3. You usually get the bulk of your rebuttals by focusing on their logic and reasoning. Does what they say make sense? Feel believable?

If not, that's an important clue. Type 4 is also fertile ground — what they say may be right, but it's not the main game. Your side still has a greater claim to winning the most significant arguments.

Here is a sample to show you the Faulty Four in operation.

Topic: *There should be mandatory jail sentences for drug crimes.*

Background: This is a "zero tolerance" approach, aimed at deterring criminals. Generally a judge has some discretion about how to sentence a guilty person. Jail, fines, community service orders, a bond — these are all options, the idea being that the punishment should fit the crime. But the judge can't do that in this debate. Anyone found guilty of a drug offence must go to jail. No allowances can be made for situations like "This is her first ever crime" or "He has five kids to look after and he did it because he was being blackmailed" or "She did it because she's an addict, and jail won't fix that." This topic wants you to argue that "If you do the crime, you do the time."

Proposition point: "If everybody knows they'll go straight to jail if they're caught buying or using drugs, fewer people will do so. That would be good for society, because drugs cause terrible damage to users and their families, and because we want to stop criminal drug rings. This plan means we solve the problems caused by drug use."

Opposition's rebuttal: Here are some possible responses, one for each of the Faulty Four:

1. **The real world is not like this.**

   "There is no convincing evidence that harsh sentences deter this type of crime. Politicians like the idea, but criminologists can't justify it. Drug criminals don't think clearly and weigh the consequences before they break the law. In fact, it can mean that more people become involved in drug crimes, because the drug rings keep having to find new dealers when their old ones are locked up."

   Their point was incorrect. This rebuttal uses the same facts to tell a truer story.

2. **Their moral position is flawed.**

   "Justice should punish criminals fairly and protect the community from harm. Sometimes that involves mercy — you can let someone go with a warning or get help for them to break their criminal connections. Their solution — even if it works — is an unjust one."

   This rebuttal challenges the morals of their argument. They've said, "We have a way to stop drug users" and you say, "Maybe you do, but it's not the right way."

3. **Their logic is flawed.**

   "Jail does not deter criminals. If it did, there would be empty jails! People who commit crimes don't expect to be caught, and they don't consider the punishment when they're deciding to break the law. They buy or use the drugs for other reasons — for example, for the money or because they're addicted. To stop them, you need to address what's causing them to do it in the first place. There's no reason to think mandatory jail leads to fewer drug crimes."

This rebuttal says their line of reasoning is mistaken. Their case misses the real cause of the problem.

4. **Their point is irrelevant.**

"This is not a debate about whether we can reduce drug crime in any way possible. This is a debate about what's a fair, reasonable, and effective way to deal with drug crimes."

This rebuttal shifts the debate by saying there's a bigger question to consider.

"Even If ..." and "Remember That ..."

These are two important techniques that allow you to say that even if the opposition's point is a good one, there is still a way to rebut it.

Use "even if" to get two rebuttals for the price of one. First, they're wrong. Second, even if they weren't wrong, there's something else that's bad about the case. For example, "First of all, computer games don't have any benefits. Second, even if they're right about the educational benefit of computer games, it still can't be good to be playing them to the exclusion of physical exercise."

Use "remember that" to agree with their point but say yours has more significance. For example, "Yes, computer games are important to today's youth, but remember, the majority of the world's youth don't have electricity, let alone computers." Or "They say our plan costs too much, but remember that we say the costs of doing nothing are even greater."

Incorrect Facts, Misleading Evidence, Life in the "Not Real" World

You would think that if a debater said something wrong, it would count against them. Alas — it is not so simple. In debater-land, a statement is true until the opposition corrects it. This means you can wind up having a debate about something that is based on an incorrect version of reality. Topics that should be about an interesting real-life problem are debated in a world of the imagination.

Let's say your team makes an untrue point. The adjudicator and audience might know that it is false even though you don't, but if your team follows through with good reasoning, and the opposition does not point out that your point was false, then your point will stand.

I once watched a debate about putting more local programs on TV. The Opposition based its case on the "fact" that we already have a whole network that shows only locally made programs. This is completely false, as a quick glance at the TV guide shows. The other side did not say so, though, and the debate went ahead based on this false claim. We had a fantasy debate about whether one local network was enough, when it should have been about whether our TV "diet" of shows made overseas is a good or bad thing.

It is more satisfying to debate real things, so you should make the effort to become a well-informed debater. This does not mean you need to have a lot of statistics and data in your memory; it means you need to understand the stories behind some common current issues and problems. However, if you find yourself in a debate on a topic you know little about, you are just going to have to accept your limits and do your best.

When not sure of the facts, frame your argument in a general way. Focus on the principles. Avoid too much specific detail, especially statistics and numbers. Stick with common sense explanations. The important thing is that your case makes sense.

In a debate about whether or not Antarctica should be mined I heard a very young team say it shouldn't, because the cost was too high — it would be at least five hundred dollars, they said. By attaching a made-up price tag, this team made it clear they didn't know what they were talking about, and their opposition picked on them for it. If they had just said, "It is extremely costly and we won't get enough for what we spend," that would have been better for their case.

Let's say you have to debate whether police should carry tasers. You don't know exactly how tasers work, or when they are used, or whether police already carry them, but you can see why there might be questions about giving police stun guns. Even knowing only that much, you could argue the case that tasers are either

- necessary protection for public safety and police self-defence; or
- risky and dangerous, because they can do unintended harm or be deliberately misused.

MS. DUFFY'S TOP TIP

Correcting factual errors is only useful if the "fact" is crucial to the other team's case. There is no need to fix it when they say something happens on Wednesdays even though you know it's Tuesdays — unless their case depends on it being Wednesdays, in which case you must correct them.

HOW TO PREPARE REBUTTALS

There are three major steps:

1. Listen to everything they say and use a cue card to note when you disagree and why. Use keywords only to trigger your recall of what they were talking about and remind you of your own line of thought. (You must keep some spare brainspace for listening during the debate, so don't try to write long notes as they talk.) Also, be on the lookout in case they are inconsistent and one speaker says something that doesn't fit with what the other person on their team is saying.
2. Next to each of their points, write why it's wrong. It doesn't need to be a perfect rebuttal — just have something to say. Ignoring a good point doesn't make it go away.
3. Second Opposition should look at the issues emerging in the debate. What "families" could they form? Combine them into two or three sensible groups. For example, you could group them according to the allocation their first speaker gave, or you could rebut all the moral arguments and then address the practical ones, or you could rebut according to the stakeholders affected. Aim to organize your rebuttals in the way that best fits this particular debate.

Here is an example of "long form" notes and two different ways of preparing rebuttal cue cards, based on those notes.

NOT BUILD HOUSES IN FIRE AREAS

Def: forest/bush areas where fires are likely

Problem! LOSING LIVES, property, danger to firefighters, 💰💰 for repairs

1 If there are no houses there are no people, = problem solved	We know people (esp farmers) are v. attached to their land, who says they won't illegally return?
2 The gov has the right — people aren't making informed decisions — save gov. fire-fighters — save gov. 💰💰	this just increases population on the EDGE of fire zones i.e. in evac. routes. Quibble! what about existing homes? You can't say that's true for EVERYONE. If it was considered, then would you allow it? Besides, people have the right to be dumb If that's the concern, make people pay a "fire tax" to live in these places

1 AFF 2ND PT

"Gov has the right" a Bad decisions b Firefighters c 💰💰	a "People aren't thinking" — not ALL — right to be dumb b These are quibbles c can be solved with a "fire tax"

1A "THIS SOLVES THE PROBLEM B/C IF THERE ARE NO HOUSES THERE ARE NO PEOPLE"

* People won't leave — love their land
  >> worse! undocumented people
* Even if they left, they'll live on outskirts
  i.e. evacuation routes

MS. DUFFY'S TOP TIP

Look back at your notes from their first speaker's allocation, when they said what they were going to prove. You should have a couple of headings. Do these match what they've said during the debate? Are they proving what they said they would prove? If they've gone off track, say so, and use it as evidence that your case is the stronger one. "Looks like they haven't been able to stick to their own points."

PRESENTING REBUTTALS PROPERLY

Introduce your rebuttal with a one-sentence summary of what they've said and announce a numbered list of two or three issues/questions/problems that you will be talking about.

Signpost your rebuttals. Say things like, "My first concern is that they try to tell us that ..." And "My second rebuttal addresses their idea that ..."; "The opposition raises three key issues ..."; "They are telling you that ... but it's not so because ..."; "It boils down to ..."; "That point rests on the belief that ..."; "Their assumption here is ..."

Work through the flaws in their case using PREP for each one. Each rebuttal must be supported with an explanation and example, but keep it brief, as you also need time to present your own case.

When you have disposed of all their weak points, say, "That concludes my rebuttals — now, on to my team's case" and move on to present your own side. This signals to the adjudicator that your team's material is now in play.

When you rebut, you must do it one hundred percent. You have to take a full-blooded opposing position. Inside your own head you are saying, "Garbage! I won't have it! This could not be more wrong!" This can be hard to do, especially if you are vigorously supporting something you do not truly agree with, but if you are not definite it

Rebuttal starts your speech. Focus on the person who just sat down, the speaker immediately before you. It is mostly their case you must demolish.

means you've admitted there's some merit in their position. There isn't. There cannot be. You will never win by saying, "They're not quite right about that." Be firm.

To help you see the other side, think of a couple of people you would never agree with. They are your new imaginary friends. By asking, "What would ... say?" you are going to be better able to see your opponent's case before they've had time to make it.

MS. DUFFY'S TOP TIP

It is fine to be emphatic, but do not be scornful or dismissive of your opponents. Do not give their case a makeover and pretend they are arguing something they are not. Humour in rebuttals is fine, if your opponents will be amused as well. Mocking, ridiculing, or making fun of what the opposition has said is not clever, it's rude.

Rebuttal Vocabulary Builder

Transitional words and phrases like these help you bring variety to your rebuttals.

Disagreeing	Giving Reasons
We don't think that	To start with
The problem with your point is that	When you consider that
The truth of the matter is	Allowing for the fact that
I'm afraid I don't agree	Considering the fact
But what about	Many people think
I doubt if	For this reason
I'd prefer	That's why
I don't agree	That's the reason why
Obviously, this is wrong	The reason is
Clearly, this doesn't take into account	Another reason it is the case that
The trouble with that point is	A further reason
This is flawed reasoning	A strong point in favour is
In contrast	
On the contrary	
On the other hand	
However	
Contrary to	

Example Rebuttals

Here are some examples for you. First, a couple of simple, straightforward ones:

Point: The government should stop funding charter schools because public schools need the money more.

Rebuttal: The government must make sure our whole population is well educated. Our future depends on it. Diversity and difference are important for achieving this. Families should be able to choose a school that best suits their children. By assisting with the cost of charter schools the government makes this possible.

Point: Athletes who take drugs should be banned for life because they're bad role models.

Rebuttal: Why does being a role model have anything to do with it? Do we sack anyone else for being a bad role model? We are holding elite athletes to an old-fashioned ideal. It's just not the way the world works.

USING PREP TO ARGUE AND TO REBUT

Here PREP is used to make a good, well-developed, and logical argument, and an equally well-developed and logical rebuttal.

The topic is *The school day should be longer*.

The Proposition might argue as follows:

Point: Over the years the school curriculum has grown so it does not fit into the school day comfortably.

Children would get a better education if they had more time at school to get through their work.

Reason/Explanation: Technological and social changes mean that kids nowadays study many more things than they used to. The demands are not the same as when the 9:00 a.m. to 3:00 p.m. school day was established. Also, children do not have to get to school in a horse-drawn vehicle or get home in time to help milk the cows, as their great-grandparents had to.

Example: We now have to learn computer science, physical education/health, and other stuff that didn't exist when the six-hour school day was invented.

Proof: So, because there is more to study, children need more time at school. The school day should be longer.

To disprove and rebut, use the same structure. You really just need to find one thing wrong with any of the statements above, but it's more convincing if there are more. For example:

Point: Yes, the curriculum has changed, but that doesn't mean it takes longer to study it. In any case, who says study has to be done at school? And don't forget we need "downtime" to recharge and be ready for more study. You need to look at the whole picture.

Reason/Explanation: The learning environment these days is quite different from what it once was, but children's physical needs as they grow up are not different. Kids are already tired after six hours at school.

There is a lot of good in having free time to regenerate, play, do sports, get involved in the community, spend time with friends and family, or just chill out. Old subjects have dropped off the curriculum, making space for modern subjects, and the internet gives us access to information whether we're at school or home or somewhere else.

Example: Our parents used to need a library to research their assignments, but we can do it online, anywhere, anytime. We no longer learn home economics like our grandmothers did.

Proof: A longer school day is not necessary. Children can manage their workload better if they are left some time to do what they want.

NOW YOU KNOW Good rebuttal is crucial to winning a debate. You can have a gold-plated case, but unless you tear down the other team's as well, you won't win.

The lesson of this chapter is that just as you have to apply REASON to your own points, you have to look for REASONS that the other team's points are wrong. To do this you should write down what they say as they say it, then look for ways their points, reasons, and examples did not support what they were trying to prove. The Faulty Four is a good place to start:

- Things don't really happen the way they say they do.
- Their arguments are morally flawed.
- Their arguments are logically flawed.
- Their arguments are not relevant, and they don't prove anything worthwhile.

Apply the PREP structure to rebuttals. Say what the flaw is (**point**), expand and explain why they're unconvincing (**reason, evidence**), and show that it does not prove their case (**proof**).

You can learn to rebut point by point, attacking what the other team has said in the order they've said it, but thematic rebuttal will do a better job. That's when you see connections between their points and bundle the ideas up and attack the lot.

You must keep notes of your rebuttals as the other team is speaking.

GIVE IT A GO! Now you try! The topic is *We should ban violent video games.* Here's the first speaker of the Proposition making a point:

"We should ban violent video games because they can lead to real-life violence. Violence is bad because victims get hurt and suffer, it creates costs to the health-care system and a feeling of unease and danger in daily life. We should do anything we can do to reduce violence.

"Video games lead to violence because when people see a depiction of some horrific things in the game, they get the idea that these are okay, normal, or entertaining. That makes it more likely that they'll go out and do them.

"Further, these games are detailed and specific. They show exact ways of hurting somebody, which people wouldn't have thought of if it wasn't for the video game — for instance, that pouring gasoline on something makes it easier to set fire to it. This actively helps people to act violently.

"Lowering the amount of violence in society is a good thing to do. We should ban violent video games."

You're the first speaker for the Opposition team, which means you're going to have to rebut this point.

Remember the Faulty Four? Time to put them into action. Try to figure out some ways you could respond to this point using each of the different faults.

The first of the Faulty Four is "The real world is not like this." How is the point we just heard wrong about the facts of real life?

The second of the Faulty Four is "Their moral position is flawed." How is the point above unfair to somebody?

The third in the Faulty Four is that "Their logic is flawed." How could you show that they've made a mistake in their reasoning? Look for any assumptions or assertions that are weak.

The fourth in the Faulty Four is that this is irrelevant. Is there a way to show that this point doesn't even matter for the debate?

I'm given some suggestions on the next two pages, but don't look at them yet — think about it for yourself first. Decide what you'd say before you look at what I've said.

"The real world is not like this."

- The evidence that video games contribute to violence is disputed. There's no definite, proven link between watching it and doing it.
- Banning would not work because people can still download illegally, and there will be a black market.

"Their moral position is flawed."

- Only some people will be violent as a result of violent video games, so it's not fair to punish all the people who play them. That's like saying that because some people drive irresponsibly, no one can have a car.
- This is unfair to the creative people (directors, writers, artists) who produce this kind of entertainment. It squashes their freedom of expression and constrains their job opportunities. That isn't fair. Nobody ever said that the authors of the Superman cartoons should be stopped in case people hurt themselves trying to fly, so why pick on these game creators?

"Their logic is flawed."

- This argument assumes that violence exists because of video games, but that's wrong. The reasoning should run the other way around:

violent people exist first and then they play
violent video games. That means that there's no
way that banning the video game would stop
them from being violent, because it didn't make
them violent to begin with.

"This is irrelevant."

- The question of whether these video games
  cause harm is beside the point. If you're
  interested in stopping violence, *do* that: use
  harsher criminal sanctions and educational
  campaigns to deter the bad behaviour.

Now choose the points you want to use and
write it out in proper debaterspeak. Use PREP and
phrases like "Even if ..." and "That's wrong because ..."
Say it out loud!

7

Speaker Roles

Speakers appear in the order below, and each has a different job to do. No single speaker is more important than any other. It's a team. All speakers have to cooperate to make the debate go well. Looking at this graphic should show you how the parts click together.

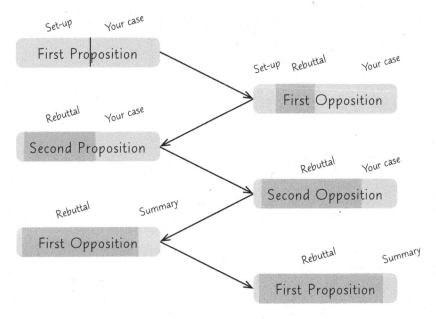

First Proposition	Explains why this is debatable, gives context. Defines and interprets the topic, clarifies the issue to prove. Presents the plan (if needed). Outlines the case and the allocation of points between speakers. Presents the most important points on their side.
First Opposition	Disagrees with the Proposition's description and proposals. Gives reasons they are unconvincing. Outlines the Opposition case and the split between speakers. Rebuts the first Proposition's case. Presents the most important points on the Opposition side.
Second Proposition	Provides the most substance for their team. Rebuts all arguments presented by the First Opposition. Adds two or three new points to the Proposition case.
Second Opposition	Provides the most substance for their team. Rebuts all arguments presented by the First and Second Proposition. Adds about two new points to the Opposition case.
First Opposition	Explains and attacks all flaws in the Proposition case. Expands and deepens Opposition criticism of the Proposition case. Summarizes own case, emphasizing the reasons it is better. Concludes the debate for the Opposition.
First Proposition	Explains and attacks flaws in the whole Opposition case. Expands and deepens Proposition's disproof of the Opposition case. Summarizes the Proposition case, emphasizing its strengths and the reasons it is better. Concludes the debate for the Proposition.

The shading shows you approximately how much of each speech is spent doing what. See how, as the debate progresses, more time is spent on rebuttal, and second speakers present less new material.

Only the first four speeches introduce fresh arguments. By the time we are at third speaker, no new material is allowed. The Reply or Rebuttal speeches' only job is to rebut the opposing case and summarize their own case.

Here's a snapshot showing the role of each speaker:

FIRST SPEAKER

First Proposition

Imagine playing a sport where one player goes out onto the field before the game and decides how long and wide the pitch will be, where the boundaries are, and where the goal posts will go.

You are like that player. That's because your main job is to clarify what the debate will be about. All three following speakers have to stick within the limits you set. A smart First Proposition can win the debate before it's even started.

First Proposition is the opening player. It's a tough spot because the audience is "cold." It's your job to give out some energy to bring the debate to life. However, as you're up first, you cannot respond to anything that has already been said. Instead, you have a tremendous opportunity to shape the entire debate. You have POWER!

Before the illusion of total control goes to your head, understand that you must use this power properly and follow certain rules. Of all the speakers in the debate, the First Proposition has the longest "to-do" list. Take your time and do it thoroughly. You must present all of the following features, in this order:

1. Introduction, Context, and Background

This is the introduction or lead-in. Start out by explaining why we are debating this topic. What's been going on in the world to make this issue a problem? Why has it happened? Is it serious? (It better be!) What harm is being caused? Who is affected? What does your team want to see instead?

Give a thorough introduction to show the audience that something must be done.

2. Definition of the Topic

When you were in the prep room you developed a simple common sense explanation of what the topic means. Deliver this clearly, calmly, and in everyday language. Clarify any unclear words and be definite about the main issues. Say what's included and what's off limits — that is, the scope of the argument.

Take your time over all this. Restate the topic clearly so there is no doubt in anyone's mind what you mean to debate. Your definition must capture the essential idea that you are going to argue about.

3. The Plan/Criteria

In a "should" debate, present your plan using words like "our solution" and "our plan."

If your debate is an "is" debate, explain the criteria you are using.

Don't go into too much specific detail — it will tie you in knots. A few sentences is plenty.

4. Allocation of Arguments or "The Case Split"

This is like the trailer or preview of your debate. The first speaker outlines, in one or two sentences, how the case will unfold. The correct way to do this is to summarize the headline idea of each point you will present, and do the same for your second speaker's points.

"Our central argument is ..."

"I will cover the issues of ... and ..."

"My second speaker will address arguments relating to ... and ..."

"The fundamental reason that we support this is ..."

5. Your Case — Substantive Matter

This is debaterspeak or shorthand for "the substance of the debate." In other words, it is the main material that you are presenting. It is not introduction, or context set-up, or rebuttal, or any other part of the debate.

The first speaker must bring out the most important two or three points in the case. Anything that is vital to winning belongs to the first speaker. It is also a good idea to put in some "pre-emptive material." This means you predict what the Opposition will say and jump in with the reason they're mistaken before they've even said it.

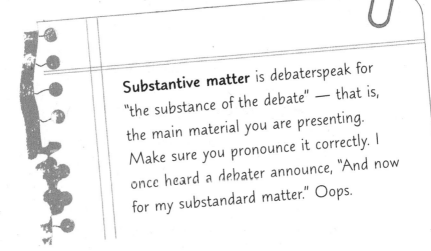

Substantive matter is debaterspeak for "the substance of the debate" — that is, the main material you are presenting. Make sure you pronounce it correctly. I once heard a debater announce, "And now for my substandard matter." Oops.

The whole Opposition team must listen very carefully to the First Proposition. Write down the definition and the allocation. That's what you have to argue against.

MS. DUFFY'S TOP TIP

Spend most of your effort on the first speaker's speech, whether you're Proposition or Opposition. The rest of the case will be there when you need it.

First Opposition

First Opposition has the shortest amount of time in the whole debate to prepare an attack. Your job is to disagree, right from the start, and then to outline your team's case.

1. Context and Background

You'll get the best debate by agreeing with the Proposition that there is a problem, but disagreeing about

- the cause and/or
- how bad the problem is (how much harm it's doing) and/or
- whether their plan will fix it. You can argue that their plan will make things worse. You can also offer a counter-plan, which is a better solution to the problem. (More on this soon.)

It's also possible to disagree by saying, "There is no problem — everything is fine as it is — just leave it all alone." This is called "maintaining the status quo." It can be a hard case to win, as debate topics are usually about something that is genuinely causing trouble in the world. I recommend you agree that there is a problem and try to use one of the other approaches.

If the First Proposition didn't explain the context (and sometimes they don't) then go ahead, you are free to do so.

2. Definition

The First Proposition has the right to define the topic. It's not usually a good idea to challenge their definition. If you do that, the debate never gets started. Like it or not, just argue the topic as they defined it. If you think it's a poor definition, say so, but accept it anyway.

If you disagree with the Proposition's definition, you can say, "We think this definition is unreasonable, but we're good debaters, so we'll go with it even though they've put us at a disadvantage." You'll have to rethink your points during the debate to incorporate their dopey definition. Doing this is easily the bravest thing you can do as a debater, and you'll almost certainly win.

The golden rule is when you're up against a bad definition, don't pretend it didn't happen. Acknowledge, adjust, and go with it. The important thing is that the debate must go on.

3. Counter-Plan

If the Proposition had a plan, your team needs to show why it won't work. Some oppositions set up a "counter-plan" (an alternative plan of action — in other words, a better way of solving the problem). You do have to prove that their approach will not solve the problem, but you don't necessarily have to propose another way of doing that. It's a judgement call for you and your team during your prep time.

4. Allocation or "The Split"

You must offer a mirror image of what the First Proposition has already done. Begin your disagreement right now. Point out that the Proposition's approach will either not solve the problem or make everything worse. Then say, in one sentence, what your team's (much better!) case is. Preview (again, in a single sentence) which points you will present and which points your second speaker will take.

And finally, begin your case.

5. Your Case — Substantive Matter

First Opposition speakers make the most important arguments against the topic.

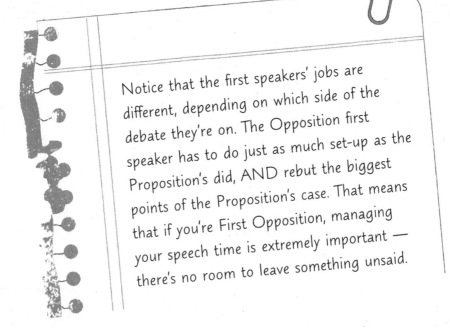

Notice that the first speakers' jobs are different, depending on which side of the debate they're on. The Opposition first speaker has to do just as much set-up as the Proposition's did, AND rebut the biggest points of the Proposition's case. That means that if you're First Opposition, managing your speech time is extremely important — there's no room to leave something unsaid.

SECOND SPEAKER

Second speakers present the bulk of the case for their team. They must keep the debate anchored and not drift away in a new direction. Your job at second is to strengthen, spread, and deepen your side's arguments. The second speaker has to secure the ground their team has already gained and expand it by adding more arguments, always keeping those arguments anchored to their first speaker's set-up.

Second Proposition

As Second Proposition you spend between a third and half of your speaking time disagreeing with the case the First Opposition has put forward. The rest of your time goes to presenting your own side.

Adjust according to what the previous speaker said. If the First Proposition has given you lots of good material to work against, then you will need more time to rebut it. If they've only given you one point and it was pretty weak, then you can devote more time to your own team's case.

Second Proposition needs one or two substantial points for their own case. Don't repeat what your first speaker has said. You must present new points.

Don't be alarmed if the adjudicator starts to look down or seems to be doing something else during your speech if you're a Second Opposition speaker. That's usually the point in the debate where they're starting to piece the debate together as a whole and look at the strategic back-and-forth, instead of just writing down what you're saying and smiling and nodding.

Second Opposition

By now quite a lot of material has been put out into the debate, and you should have plenty of arguments to rebut. Your speech should be about half rebuttal and half new material to support your own team's case. You need one or two substantial points for your own side.

When the Second Opposition speaker sits down, that completes the case, so be sure all your points have been completely covered.

REBUTTAL SPEECHES

After the second speakers have made their speeches, the first speakers make rebuttal/summary speeches. These speakers are only allowed to rebut and summarize; they must not introduce any significant new arguments. It is fine to retell the story and represent the case while elaborating, expanding, and explaining what has already been argued, but the rebuttal speeches should not send the debate in a new direction. Quite simply, it's not fair to do that when the other team has no come-back.

At this point, first speakers deal with the whole story of the debate. They should focus on the main clashes — the issues that emerged as the big ones.

Summary and Rebuttal Speeches

The first speaker in each team makes a second, shorter speech that summarizes and refutes the other side's case *overall*. In three person teams, this role is taken by the third member.

Ensure you've attacked all the opposing team's arguments. Focus on the big picture, using phrases like "What they're really saying is ..." or "They're trying to tell us ... But ..."

Look for the three main issues in their case (for some reason, there are just about always three main issues). If you can't see three issues easily, think about the framework you used in prep (the problem, the cause, the harm, the solution, and the plan for fixing it) and re-use it. Or consider our most basic "case development" questions:

- Why don't their arguments solve the problem?
- How are they being unfair or unjust?
- Which stakeholders will be worse off?

Your challenge is to avoid repetition. You need to use different phrases. Say things like "We already told you that ... What I'm going to add is that ..." It's also a good opportunity to add fresh examples and more detailed explanations of the faults in their reasoning.

Then restate the core of your own case in a summary form, once again emphasising the major issues. Remember not to present major new points of your own.

If you are First Proposition, your rebuttal speech is the last speech of the debate. YOU get the last word. Your arguments are the ones that will be left ringing in the ears of the judge. You'll do this well if you can listen to a whole debate's worth of arguments and rebut them in themes, without doubling up. This is often where the feistiest, punchiest debater does well, and it's certainly a good spot for someone who likes the adrenalin rush of thinking on your feet. Focus on the big picture. The best rebuttal speakers understand the shape of the argument as a whole.

Review everything that's wrong with what the Opposition said. Look for the theme of the debate, the central ideas and major areas of disagreement. Open up the issues behind what you've been saying. Then pivot back to everything that's convincing in what your side said.

Points of Information

Many — but not all — styles of debating expect you to interject to challenge the person speaking. This is called a "Point of Information." You can only do it at specified times (not in rebuttal speeches and not during the opening minute or so of any speech), and you don't just yell it out. It's like in class — you stand up politely and announce "Point of Information" or hold your hand out as if you were signalling the bus to stop. The speaker has to accept or decline your request. When they finish what they're saying, they can turn to you, and you ask your question BRIEFLY. You must not be long-winded. They can also decline to answer you: by waving at you to sit down, saying "no thank you," or "not now." If they do this, you have to sit down. The better you get at debating, the more important it is to offer and accept these interjections. The judges see them as evidence of skill. "Give two and take two" is the rough rule.

 NOW YOU KNOW Every speaker has their own special job to do, and winning the debate depends on everyone doing their job. First speakers set up what's going to happen in the debate and give the most important points. Second speakers are like defence warriors who back up their side's case, give some more points, and attack the other team's. The first speakers then tear down the other side's case and summarize their side's argument. Remember that your job will be a bit different in each position depending on whether you're the Proposition or the Opposition.

8

A Debate from Start to Finish

WHAT TO DO IN PREP

Handling prep time well is mission critical. On it depends the success of your debate! It is going to become one of the most exciting and stimulating times in your life. You are going to look forward to it. Time in the prep room is satisfying and fun. Yes, prep time can be stressful, but with practice you will become great, and the teamwork you learn in this high-pressure situation will stay with you for a long time.

Remember you're in this together. Support each other. You all need to stay focused and serious about managing the time effectively. And breeeeaaathe. It'll all be over soon.

Keys to Success

Do

- Appoint someone to watch the time.
- Know each other's strengths and use them. If someone is good at shaping arguments, let them. If someone has a great general knowledge, use it. If someone is a great note taker, get help from them.

Don't

- Be silly, throw tantrums, hold off-topic conversations, or have hissy fits. They are as stressed as you.
- Allow distractions — stay on the job.
- Be rude rather than constructive.
- Turn up without pens, pencils, erasers, markers, cue cards, and paper.

Time Management

To use your one hour prep time properly follow this formula (if you have less than or more than one hour, adjust it):

1. Five minutes of silent brainstorming. Get your own ideas onto a piece of paper, using a mindmap or point form. Prepare the whole case. If your teammate is sucked up by a hurricane on the way

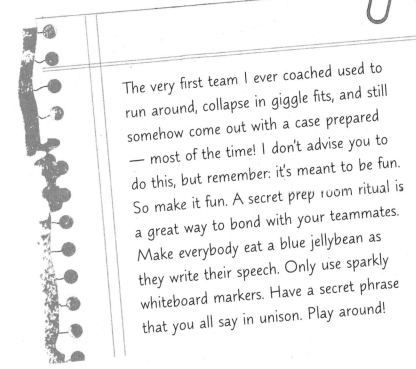

The very first team I ever coached used to run around, collapse in giggle fits, and still somehow come out with a case prepared — most of the time! I don't advise you to do this, but remember: it's meant to be fun. So make it fun. A secret prep room ritual is a great way to bond with your teammates. Make everybody eat a blue jellybean as they write their speech. Only use sparkly whiteboard markers. Have a secret phrase that you all say in unison. Play around!

to the debate room, your piece of paper from the brainstorm would still carry an approach to the whole case.

2. Five minutes to share and splash points up on the whiteboard or blackboard.

3. Five minutes to sort and critique these points, to look for the themes and threads that tie the issues together.

4. If you are the Proposition: five minutes deciding the definition and plan/criteria. If you are the

Opposition: five minutes predicting what the definition and plan will be and preparing your response.

5. Fifteen minutes case construction: choose the five best points, put them in order of importance, and allocate them. Work out points, sub-points, and what examples will be used. Forecast what the opposition will say and adjust accordingly.

6. Fifteen minutes to write speech outlines. Sit quietly writing your own arguments and rebuttals out.

7. Some spare moments at the end.

PRO TIP

It's important to have a time management plan in prep, but don't fuss and micromanage what happens every minute — this just creates stress and panic. Panic in prep is the *worst* thing. Let the time manager speak up every five minutes or so, to keep everyone focused and moving forward.

Oscar, grade ten

Three Golden Rules

1. Stay Calm

Stress can make us panic and not think straight. You know how you forget all the math you've learned once you're in an exam? AAAAGGHHHH! You can make mistakes in the prep room just as easily as stupid mistakes in an exam. Fortunately, this problem is one of the easiest to solve.

- Bring some food! Chocolate expands your brainpower.
- Take a deep breath. You'll lose two seconds, max, and you'll be amazed at how much more clearly you think afterward.
- Be nice. These are your friends.

2. Know Your Roles

If you each have a job, it makes things run smoothly. But if you're both grabbing for the whiteboard marker and disagreeing over the points your teammate is proposing, you'll wind up arguing with each other — not the opposing team.

You could make one person the "whiteboard jockey" — the person with the best handwriting, who can write up all the arguments you've thought of. Split up these roles: the "mediator," who controls the flow of conversation and who says whose turn it is to speak; the "rebuttal preparer," who thinks of everything the opposition could say and writes some rebuttals to have handy before you go in; and someone in charge of watching the time.

3. Stick to Timing

It's okay to choose whatever timing you like, but once you've chosen it, stick to it like glue. There's nothing worse than running out of time.

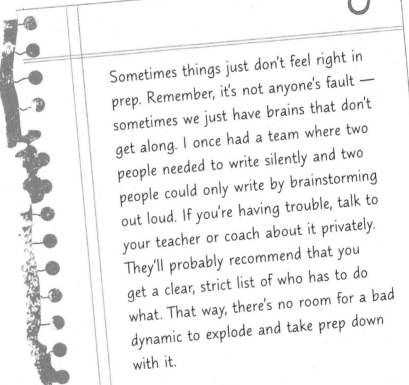

Sometimes things just don't feel right in prep. Remember, it's not anyone's fault — sometimes we just have brains that don't get along. I once had a team where two people needed to write silently and two people could only write by brainstorming out loud. If you're having trouble, talk to your teacher or coach about it privately. They'll probably recommend that you get a clear, strict list of who has to do what. That way, there's no room for a bad dynamic to explode and take prep down with it.

174

Skillful Scribbling

Getting your case onto cards or a sheet of paper is a skill in itself.

Some students write their case on a large sheet of paper and put it flat on a desk in front of them. That's how older debaters do it, and some students like to be able to see the whole case at a glance. However, it ties the speaker down to one spot and means they must look down a lot, rather than speaking out to the audience.

It's more common for debaters to use cue cards. These mean you can move about, look at the audience, and use gestures more easily.

Which ever one you use, you need to make good notes and have a system for following the debate. Here is one approach.

Shorten the Words

Develop a personal shorthand for frequently used words; for example:

- Definition can become *Def* or *D*
- Background is *b/g*
- Harm is *H*
- First point is *P1*
- First rebuttal is *Reb1*
- First Proposition becomes *PropA*
- Example is *eg*
- Reason is *R*

- Because can become *b/c* or *bec*
- Therefore is *t/f*
- Use math symbols such as = equals, ≠ is not equal to, > greater than, < less than, ∴ therefore, ∵ because, ~ similar to
- Leave out the vowels, or just use the first few letters of the word

Outline Only

Just use key words, never whole sentences. Leave out "and" and "the," and use your abbreviations, arrows, shortcut words, and symbols to help you go fast.

- Note the headline points close to the left-hand side of the page or card.
- Under that, but indented away from the left side, use single words to note what the point is about. Look at page 141 to see an example.

Number Your Cards

This is crucial! If you happen to drop all your cue cards (and it happens to many debaters), you need to be able to get them into the right order quickly. Also, make the final card obvious, in case you have to get to it in a hurry because time is running out. Use a different coloured pen, draw a big stripe on the edge of it, or tear the corner off — anything to make it stand out.

NOW YOU KNOW You have a limited amount of time in the prep room to get everything done. That can be stressful. But if you follow this chapter's golden rules, you'll be okay. Watch the time, stay calm, and work together. Don't forget: the other team has just as little time as you do.

ROOM SET-UP

The debate room has to be set up in a certain way. A chairperson and a timekeeper, who sit at the front of the room in between the two teams, manage the debate. The adjudicator, who sits at the back of the room, judges it.

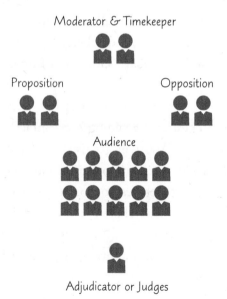

Moderator & Timekeeper

Proposition   Opposition

Audience

Adjudicator or Judges

177

The timekeeper will issue a warning (like ringing a bell or slapping the table) to let a speaker know it's time to finish. When the speaker sits down, there is a pause until the adjudicator is ready to hear the next speaker. When the adjudicator signals by nodding, the moderator introduces the next speaker and the debate continues.

ON YOUR FEET!

Be ready. When the adjudicator gives the nod and you are introduced, you need to bounce out into the debate with enthusiasm. Don't keep writing as you stand up, flap your arms, or go, "Wait, wait!" You need to appear as though you're in charge.

Gather up your cards (make sure they're numbered and in the right order) and walk confidently around the desks to the front centre. Stop there. Look at everyone in the room, smile, and say, "Good morning/afternoon/evening."

Do not be surprised if you feel like burying your chin in your chest and avoiding eye contact — this is a normal reaction. You will get used to that feeling. It passes after the first minute or so of your speech, and after your first few debates you probably won't experience it at all. (See "Nuke Those Nerves," starting on page 207, which talks about the "fight or flight" response. The stress can actually become a thrill, like going fast on your bike or playing in a final.)

At the end of your speech say: "Thank you," count "one, two" silently to yourself, and then return to your seat. Don't flee the scene and rush away. When you get back to your seat, do not roll your eyes, or flop down dramatically, or make a show of going "Phew!" and throwing the cards in an imaginary bin. Keep your game face on. Remain composed and attentive till the debate is finished.

At the very end of the debate, you might shake hands with your opponents while you are waiting to hear the adjudication.

What to Say and How to Say It

You are judged partly on your manner, so you need to be worth listening to. Good speakers can be heard and understood. They speak clearly and sound natural. Imagine you are talking to an adult you really like. Talk to your audience just as you would to a favourite teacher — it will make you sound just formal enough, not too stuffy and stagy. Use your normal vocabulary.

Your voice, face, eyes, and body should work together to make what you say impressive and convincing. It's especially important that your voice indicates the most important parts of the debate. So don't hold back when you talk about the harms or describe the pain suffered by the stakeholders. Vary your expression and create a mood that works with your line of argument.

Let your speech live. If you are interested in what you have to say, that will come through in your voice, and your excitement will be transmitted to your listeners. Vary the pace, tone, and colour of your voice, and let your emotions come through. That makes you sound lively and interesting.

Most people say "er" and "um" when they start out as speakers. These hesitations give you time to think. With practice, you will become more polished and these fillers should disappear.

To deliver a speech with style:

- Keep your eyes on the audience.
- Use a loud and clear voice, with variety in your tone.
- Do not speak too quickly.
- Stand straight and strong.
- Address the audience. Don't talk to your opposition — you're never going to convince THEM!

Structuring Your Debate Speeches

You won't be surprised to hear that speeches have a beginning (or introduction), a middle (rebuttal and substantive matter) and an end (conclusion). You need to move through the components of the speech smoothly and let your adjudicator know which bit you're up to.

Using Signposts

Signposts are verbal headings that tell the listener what section of your speech you are in. Some of them help you travel from one section of your speech to another. Using signposts highlights the fact that you're doing what you're meant to and not leaving anything out.

It's important that you're clear about which part of your job you are doing and that the audience is clear on that, too. It's very important that the adjudicator knows exactly what part of your speech you are up to — it enables her or him to follow your case properly and keep proper track of what you are doing. For that reason you must use signposts.

The **introduction** can just be a plain "good morning/afternoon/evening." You do not have to greet everyone in the room, or repeat the topic, or say what speaker you are. Just get down to business.

Next you need a **lead-in sentence** that explains what the audience is about to listen to. This sentence varies according to your position in the debate.

The First Proposition should say, "This house would …," This house believes that …," or "This house supports …"

First Opposition could say, "The Opposition takes a different view of this issue …"

Second Proposition would open with, "The Opposition wants you to believe that … But we say … Here is my rebuttal of their case."

Second Opposition could say, "We disagree with the Proposition in two big ways …"

The First Proposition would then start with "The debate today had three main issues …"

First Opposition would then say something very similar.

As your speech proceeds, label what you are doing quite explicitly: "Here is my first point of rebuttal … And now for my second point of rebuttal … Now here is my team's case. My first point is that … My second point is … In conclusion …" — and so on.

Conclude gracefully by summarizing your argument and restating your side of the topic. Don't tell the audience that you've convinced them or won the debate — you don't know that. You can end with "Thank you" and sit down.

Using Cue Cards

While speaking, you need to manage your cue cards. Most debaters have dropped the lot at least once in their career — this is one reason it's important to number them! Just smile cheerfully, pick them up, and sort them out. It is poor practice to read from your cards. Use them just to prompt you. Keep your eyes on the audience. Hold your cards in one hand if you can. You then have the other one free to make gestures and emphasize what you have to say.

MS. DUFFY'S TOP TIP

Make sure your last card — the one that includes a summary of your case — stands out. Put a highlight stripe on it, turn the corner down or tear it off, or write it in a different colour. That way, if you run over time and need to finish, you can find it fast.

Keep an Eye on the Time

Wear a watch or get a timer. And look at it! When you are debating you will be focused only on what you are saying, and it is very easy to lose track of time. You can easily say more than you need to about a particular point and before you know it the warning bell is ringing and you've barely begun your case.

Don't try talking at double speed after the first warning. Just choose the most significant point you have left and deliver that one.

We've learned already how much time goes into the different parts of each person's speech. The older you get, the longer your speeches will be, but these proportions stay the same. It is important to stick to them. The more you debate, the more you will get the feel of how long you've been speaking for.

> **MS. DUFFY'S TOP TIP**
>
> If you hear the first warning and you find you don't have time to finish, don't speed up to try and fit everything in. Choose the most significant point you have left, and present it at your normal pace.

Managing Nerves

You will be nervous. I repeat: YOU WILL BE NERVOUS. Everyone is. Debating is scary. It's a competition. You are standing alone in front of an audience and an opposing team. You have not been able to prepare and rehearse your speech because (unless you're First Proposition) a good part of it is based on what the last person said just a few minutes ago. This is stressful! Pat yourself on the back for even giving it a go — most people would rather not.

Understanding your own brand of nerves will make them easier to deal with. All sorts of things are possible: you might sweat, stammer, or shake. Your voice might crack or go hoarse. You might speed up. Your mind might go blank. Twisty tummies are common. Perhaps you're a blusher. Or a "happy wanderer," strolling about the floor and waving your hands. You might even be one of those unlucky debaters who stands up

There is a competition in the U.S. where quick talk is considered a good thing. Fasten your seatbelt and Google "Chicago speed debaters."

and needs to vomit. (If so, just say, "Excuse me" and get to the bathroom quickly. In time, your lunch will learn to stay where it belongs.) I have seen all of these things. I have even seen a couple of speakers faint, come round, and go back to their speech.

Just remember that nerves are normal. Accept them and learn to manage them. Get a teacher or parent, someone you trust and feel comfortable with, to watch you in action and let you know honestly how your nerves are coming across. If your school allows it, get them to record you. Check out "Nuke Those Nerves" in the public speaking section of this book (starting on page 207), where you'll find suggestions for helping yourself to stay calm and for making sure that nerves, while affecting how you feel, don't affect what you say or do.

KNOW YOUR NERVES

Everyone's nerves show in a particular way. Whether you're a blusher, a shaker, a stammerer, or something else, the more familiar you are with your brand of nerves, and the more you accept them and learn to manage them, the easier debating will be.

TAKING NOTES WHILE THOSE ALL AROUND YOU TALK!

By the time the debate starts you will have a set of cue cards that contain your speaking points. As the debate unfolds, you need to make notes on what your opponents say so that you can counteract it.

This is a high-pressure situation. Writing and listening at the same time puts a big demand on your "personal bandwidth." It takes a lot of concentration. Note-taking is a vital skill, and to succeed as a debater you must master it.

You need a system for keeping a well-organized record of the case as it unfolds.

The Equipment

At a junior level, you can start just with cue cards. Use two piles, one for "they say" and the other for "we say" (you should have prepared this pile in the prep room). Try hard not to write sentences. Pick one or two words that will remind you what they said and what you plan to say in response.

As soon as you are comfortable doing this, move on to this method.

All debaters should have **paper** as well as **cue cards**. You need a **pen** (that works — you'd be amazed how many students turn up without one), and a **highlighter or different coloured pen** as well.

The large paper is for noting down the opposition's case. This sheet becomes a one-page summary of what

MS. DUFFY'S TOP TIP

Make yourself a debating kit. Park everything you need — an electronic timer, cue cards, paper, pens, whiteboard markers, and highlighters — in a big zip-lock bag. Your personal needs go in there as well: glasses, hair ties, bobby pins, and an emergency chocolate. Zip it all up at the debate's end and you're ready for the next one.

they say and what you plan to say in response. It can be a messy, scribbly sheet — you will not speak off it. It is good brainwork to get used to seeing their debate as one whole thing on a single sheet, rather than a set of separate points chopped up and physically located on different cue cards. The best debaters kill their opposition's entire argument, rather than taking it apart point by point. This is easier if you can see it in one glance.

The cue cards are for what you personally are going to say. The cue cards go out onto the floor with you, the sheet stays behind on the desk. The highlighter (or different coloured pen) is so you can neatly cross out the opposition's points on the sheet when you have transferred a response to them onto your cue cards.

How to Outline Their Case

Follow the same procedure you already used for your own case. Look at page 141 for examples.

- Note down their signposts and headline points close to the left-hand side of the page or card.
- Under that, but indented away from the left side, use single words to note what the point is about.
- On the right-hand side of the page or card, note reminders of what you want to say in response.

Once the Debate Begins ...

1. The first thing you must do is write down the
    definition and allocation that the first speaker
    gives. Put that on a separate piece of paper, which
    you park on the desk in front of you. It is the plan
    for the debate. Everything that is said in the debate
    should fit into this outline. Refer to it all the time
    — ask yourself, "Are they proving their case as they
    said they would?" "Are we proving our case as we
    said we would?"
2. On your paper "case" sheet, write down the
    headlines and points that each speaker makes, and
    make a note of your response.
3. Transfer the points you will make to your cue
    cards. Cross each point off the sheet when you've
    done so. Check that you haven't overlooked
    anything before you stand up to speak. Obviously,
    this has to be done very fast!

Remember, you must quickly move from the big
page to the cue cards so they are ready when it's time
to go.

Good notes capture the main issue and remind you
of the argument that was used to support it, as well as
your own response.

PRO TIP

There's no need to preserve their exact words — use notes that make the concept stick in your head. However, using the same labels they've used means you'll be speaking the same language as they did, and the adjudicator will hear clearly that you are addressing their arguments.

Eleanor, coach

TEAM TABLE MANNERS

The rule is simple: no talking at the table. While the debate rages, you will get bright ideas, see a new angle, or think of a rebuttal, for yourself or for someone else. Fight the instinct to tell your teammate what you just thought of. You must listen. You want to tell your teammate something? Whisper it softly, or write it down.

It is not okay to talk. It is okay to pass a cue card. That's *pass* a cue card. They are not missiles or paper planes.

If you are using the case-on-a-page described above, you have a single sheet on the desk that you can share in order to map the case as it unfolds. By the end, the two teams will have a complete outline of the whole debate, including points of information and possible rebuttals. The Reply speaker thus has an easy reference to check before speaking.

While the debate is on you should not communicate by sign language or vigorous nodding with anyone else. Spoken or body language that distracts from the person speaking is the debating equivalent of trash talking.

MS. DUFFY'S TOP TIP

Advice to parents: If you get to watch your child debate, it's great for both of you. Remember, however, that every parent in the room has a child champion in the making. We're all besotted with our own kids, but we need to rein ourselves in. Beaming, nodding, giving them a thumbs up, or filming or photographing them will draw attention away from the team as a whole. Your boy- or girl-wonder might even be embarrassed or put off by it, and others in the room may find it distracting as well. Best keep a low profile.

NOW YOU KNOW In this section we've learned how a debate operates. We've covered the room set-up, what equipment you need, how to behave so that you hear the opposition, take notes, stay organized, and get your speech out the way you want it. You've had some hints on taming any butterflies, speaking to time, and keeping a record.

A debate is a high-pressure time. When you have done a few, this will all become much easier.

THE MODERATOR, TIMEKEEPER, AND ADJUDICATOR

The moderator and timekeeper play a very important part in making the debate go smoothly. They make sure the room is set up properly, and they write the topic on the board so everyone knows what is being debated.

The Moderator

The moderator welcomes the audience and introduces each speaker and, at the end, the adjudicator. During the debate, the moderator must watch for the signal from the adjudicator that they are ready to listen to the next speaker.

Sample Moderator's Script

I welcome you to the _____ round of the _____ debating competition.

This debate is between (name school) and (name school).

The Proposition team, from (school) is

1st speaker _____

2nd speaker _____

Coach _____

The Opposition team, from (school) is

1st speaker _____

2nd speaker _____

Coach _____

The adjudicator for this debate is _____.

Each constructive speaker may speak for ___ minutes. There will be a warning at ___ minutes, and the time-keeper will stand at ___ minutes to indicate that the speaker's time has expired. Rebuttal speeches will be ___ minutes.

The topic for this debate is _____

The 1st Proposition Speaker, _____ , will begin the debate.

The 1st Opposition Speaker, _____ , will begin their case.

The 2nd Proposition Speaker, _____ , will continue their case.

The 2nd Opposition Speaker, _____ , will continue their case.

The 1st Opposition Speaker, _____ , will conclude their case.

The 1st Proposition Speaker, _____ , will conclude the debate.

[WAIT till you get a nod from the adjudicator.]

The adjudicator will now deliver the adjudication and announce the result of this debate.

[The adjudicator comes forward and speaks. When they finish there will be applause. Let it die down, then stand up.]

A team member from (school) will now congratulate the winners.

A member of the winning team will now respond.

That concludes this debate. Thank you for coming. Please join us for refreshments at _____.

[If there are any!]

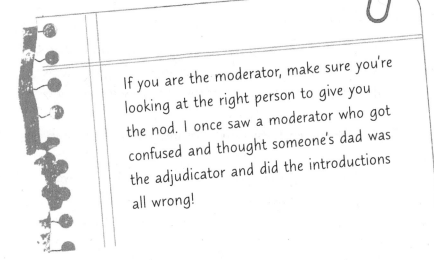

If you are the moderator, make sure you're looking at the right person to give you the nod. I once saw a moderator who got confused and thought someone's dad was the adjudicator and did the introductions all wrong!

The Timekeeper

The timekeeper has the important job of warning the speaker that they are getting near the end of their time and of letting them know when time is up and they must sit down.

Each competition has its own rules about how long to speak, but generally there is a single DING or slap to warn the speaker that a minute is left and then a double slap or DING DING when it's time to stop. After a fifteen-second grace period, the timekeeper stands up and tells the speaker to sit down. It can be quite daunting to do this to someone who is speaking, but be confident when you perform these roles, or the debate will not be well run.

All About Adjudicating

The adjudicator awards the debate to the team that has been most convincing, according to the principles described in this book. Their role is a bit different from the referee or umpire in other competitions, because there are no goals, or runs to count, and no finish line for one team to reach first.

They look at the points each team made, how well supported they were, the logic of the case, and how well that compared to the case made by the other side. They focus on reasons. They will take a detailed look at the logic of your arguments.

They look at the whole debate before they make their decision. One single thing is not going to lose it or win it for you.

During the debate they signal (by nodding) when it's time for the next speaker to start. As the debate progresses, if the moderator or the timekeeper makes a mistake or gets lost, the adjudicator may say something to help out. They may also ask for "order" if anyone is being disruptive by talking, signing, or making faces. This is serious — don't resume the bad behaviour. An adjudicator should not have to ask for order twice.

How They Do It

The adjudicator takes notes during the debate. Sometimes they use a form, or they may just make notes on a piece of paper. They log the arguments and keep notes on things they can say in feedback at the end. In some competitions they may fill in a formal result sheet that looks something like the one below.

An adjudicator has to leave their opinions outside the debating room. They are not supposed to "enter the debate," which is debaterspeak for allowing their own ideas, beliefs, and knowledge to shape their view of how well a case is being argued. They should judge according to what is said and how persuasive it would be to a reasonable, ordinary person.

Adjudication Sheet

Round: _____   Venue: _____   Age group: _____

Topic: _____

Adjudicator: _____

Proposition School:	Opposition School:
1st Speaker: Score:	1st Speaker: Score:
2nd Speaker: Score:	2nd Speaker: Score:
1st Speaker Rebuttal: Score:	1st Speaker Rebuttal: Score:
Proposition Team Total:	Opposition Team Total:

Overall comments:

Delivering the Result

At the end of the debate, the adjudicator finishes their notes and gives the moderator a nod. The moderator introduces the results. The adjudicator stands up and delivers them. They give a short summary of the debate and say, in a few words, what they thought the main issues were and how the debate played out. They will tell you who won and lost and WHY. They will give reasons!

Debaters should then speak to the adjudicator individually to get personal feedback. Be prepared to wait around after the debate and hear what they have to say. Make sure you take away a practical tip or piece of advice that you can keep in mind for your next debate.

Adjudicating is an art as well as a science, and different adjudicators might judge the same debate differently. That's hard to take if you're on the losing side, but it's a fact of life. As one very experienced adjudicator once said, "I know I can only take half the room with me."

Losing Gracefully

It is poor form to challenge the adjudicator. If you think you've lost unfairly, don't show it. Trust me on this. Do not display your feelings. Graciousness and good sportsmanship are qualities that will set you apart. Here is the chance to develop them.

Later, in private, it is a good idea to debrief as a team and come to terms with the decision and also take on board any advice for what you could have done better. Different people like different styles of debating, and one of the skills you need to develop is how to be appealing to a wide range of listeners.

You Be the Adjudicator

One of the very best ways to learn about debating is to practise adjudicating a debate.

Watch a debate in your own age group, or one that's not too much older than you, and pretend you are the adjudicator. See for yourself how easy (or hard) it is to follow what's being said. Keep an accurate record.

Split your page in two. Note what they say in the left and your comments on the right so that you can give the speakers feedback.

 NOW YOU KNOW The moderator, timekeeper, and adjudicator each has their own job, just like you do.

The moderator and timekeeper present the debate in a professional manner and make sure you all stick to the timing rules.

The adjudicator's job is a bit like yours: they have to use reasoning to work out who won and then make a speech and explain and justify their decision.

A Debate from Start to Finish

Debating wouldn't work without these people, just like it wouldn't work without you, so remember to treat them nicely. Besides, listening to them is a crucial part of becoming a better debater.

Part 2

PUBLIC SPEAKING

9

Introducing Public Speaking

Let's start by dispelling some myths.

Lots of people say they're paralyzed by the idea of public speaking. They say it's scarier than snakes, spiders, or their grumpy great-uncle with the overgrown garden and the large snarly dogs. Well, here's what I say: don't ever think that public speaking is something you can't do. It's just that most people are not used to it. Have you tried it? All you need is some practice. Sure, the situation makes special demands, but the basics are not that different from what you do every day. You talk to your family, friends, teachers, parents (your own and others') and to store clerks, bus drivers, and heaps of other people, all the time with perfect ease. You already know how to think on your feet and speak. You just need to get accustomed to having a larger audience and to being the one who is listened to. Trust me, you can do it. And you should do it.

Public speaking is a skill you will use now and in the future. Speaking well in public prepares you for positions of responsibility and visibility. Speak up, speak well, and all sorts of opportunities will be open to you. Maybe you already long for the limelight and the applause. Good for you! Or maybe you are the quiet type and are doubtful about public speaking. Bear in mind that quiet people are some of the most rewarding ones to listen to, because they are so thoughtful, and they consider things deeply.

WHAT'S INVOLVED?

Public speaking is all about you. What *you* think, what *you've* noticed, what *you* want to share with others. It gives you a chance to speak on just one subject, and allows you time to prepare thoroughly, exercise creativity, and go deep into your theme. You can take your time and linger. It's as if you get to turn over the rocks on a path and examine each one closely before you put it back and move on to the next one. Then you make some observations and tell others all about it.

Unlike in debating, there's no need to argue or prove something is right. You *do* get to choose what position to take, and you are free to observe, discuss, reflect, describe, and present your own point of view.

In public speaking, the *way* you present is just as important as *what* you present. It's a performance. In public speaking, engaging your listeners and being a really classy verbal communicator is the main game.

Your choice of words, your connection to the audience, the way you use your voice and the way you stand, move, and gesture are all very important.

Competitions

Speaking competitively is excellent experience. There are several major competitions, and they are run by different organizations (see page 252 for more details). Each has a slightly different format. They usually ask for shorter speeches (4–6 minutes) for the under-fifteen age group and longer ones (8–10 minutes) in the senior school years.

Other Occasions

You don't have to be in a competition to do public speaking — there are lots of other ways to get some experience.

- In almost every subject in high school you are expected to do an oral presentation as part of your assessment.
- If you are in a leadership position — for example class president or vice-president — or if you're on the Student Council, you will likely speak in public, either to your school assembly or by representing your school in the community.
- If you're good at something you might have to speak because you've won a prize!

- There are also private occasions that you might speak at: a special birthday, for instance, or at a family, club, or community occasion.

This section of the book guides you through the sort of occasions you will meet in your public speaking life at school and gives you "recipes" for making speeches that suit the occasion well.

NUKE THOSE NERVES!

I've promised you that you can do public speaking, but I know you might still be anxious about it, so let's begin with a short explanation of how to deal with that anxiety. Once you're feeling more confident, you'll be able to focus on how to write and deliver a great speech.

For most people, public speaking is stressful. To paraphrase comedian Jerry Seinfeld, "If it's true that more people fear public speaking than dying, then most of the people at a funeral would rather be in the box than giving the eulogy."

Really? THAT stressful?

Well, maybe. Even the most experienced speakers suffer nerves. It's called *glossophobia*, which comes from the Greek word for tongue. Deep down, it's a fear of making embarrassing mistakes. It's a misplaced fear because — unless you are the president — most audiences are very supportive. Very few audiences (and in my experience, none at all) are hoping you'll fall flat on your face, fumble your words, or find you've forgotten to do up your fly. They are forgiving. They want you to succeed.

The trouble is, your body doesn't know that. Your body responds to stresses like speeches, exams, or being sent to the Principal in exactly the same way. It senses danger. You get ready for fight or flight. When you get up in front of a crowd, and you have many eyes upon you and nowhere to hide, your brain says "You're *not safe here* … You need to *get away!*" and floods you with adrenalin to help make your exit a speedy one.

Unfortunately, you can't choose the "flight" path. Depending on your personality this can be exhilarating. Or it may be exhausting, an ordeal. You might feel all fired up, in your element; or your palms might sweat, your throat croaks, your knees are jelly, and your heart pounds. Afterwards, you might suffer the "adrenalin hangover," and feel exhausted and drained, as anyone does after an ordeal.

There are only two things you can do: accept it and manage it.

If you realize that it's normal to be nervous, you will spare yourself a lot of worry. After that, it's a matter of knowing how to help yourself when the nervousness strikes.

Ways to Cope

Speaking is like learning an instrument or playing a sport — it takes repetition and practice. And exactly as for sport and music (and exams and other testing situations), being well prepared makes a big difference. If you are well practised, nerves may affect how you feel but are less likely to affect what you do.

Nervousness is an internal state. The audience doesn't know your inner workings. If you could see yourself, you'd probably find you look perfectly okay. They won't even have noticed you're on edge.

Some simple tips will help you stay calm:

- Before you speak, work off excess anxiety with some exercise. Go for a run, walk the dog, see how many sit-ups you can do.
- Close to time, stretch and release your face and jaw a few times.
- When you're about to start, settle yourself with deep, regular breathing. Breathe in and ... wait. Breathe out s-l-o-w-l-y and ... wait. Do this ten times (don't hyperventilate, please) and you will feel more in control.

Anxiety drops after you start. Once you get through the introduction, you should find the rest is easier. Below are some more tips.

MS. DUFFY'S TOP TIPS

- If you're a heavy sweater, be ready to dab with a folded handkerchief.
- Don't hold a sheet of paper in a shaky hand. Use cards instead.
- Get trembling hands under control by loosely clasping them in front of you.
- A sea of faces is less scary when you eyeball people one at a time. Try it — it's not so strange as you'd expect.
- If you do dry up or go blank or stumble, it's always okay to take a minute. Smile at the audience, who will not mind your moment of difficulty, and restart when you're ready.

Figure out what scares you. Try asking yourself, "What's the worst that can happen?," then list how you can prevent that thing from happening. (The words "avoid public speaking" are not allowed on this list.) People usually fear speaking in public because they believe they can't do it. Proving to yourself that you can do it will help.

LESSONS FROM A WISE OLD GREEK

About 2,300 years ago, Aristotle, a mega-famous thinker, wrote down three keys to being a powerful speaker. If you've heard the terms **oratory** or **rhetoric**, that is what he was talking about. Believe it or not, his ideas still work.

He called the three keys to public speaking **ethos**, **pathos**, and **logos**, but let's switch to modern English and call them "credibility, connection, and content."

These have become known as the Pillars of Public Speaking. Do not forget them! They are the engine of every presentation. You need them the way a runner needs legs. Let's look at them more closely.

The Three Pillars of Public Speaking

Ethos or Credibility

When you have credibility, people will respect what you are saying. You are believable because of who you are, what you know, and the soundness of what you have to say.

In the adult world, **credibility** partly depends on the speaker's role or position. This gives them authority. If Bill Gates talks to me about how he's eliminating poverty in Africa I might believe it, because he's one of the richest people on earth, and he spends a LOT on worthwhile projects. If you claimed to be doing the same thing, I might not be so easily convinced. As a school student, you haven't had time to develop this sort of credibility. However, you can still present a credible point of view. Your background, personality, and your life experience are valuable resources. You should use them in your speeches.

Pathos or Connection

You can find the word "**pathos**" inside our modern words "empathy" and "sympathy." Pathos is emotion, the rapport with the audience. It's important because it gets people on your side. Motivational speakers, politicians, and salespeople depend heavily on pathos. It's the key that a speaker turns to unlock the audience's support, interest, and even their cold hard cash. When you **connect** with people, when their feelings are engaged, they feel stirred up, motivated, excited. When you leave a presentation going "WOWWWWW!" the speaker has probably played the pathos card. Think of your favourite ad at the moment — I bet it excites you somehow. And remember the Roger Federer example? (See page 42.) Pathos!

Logos or Content

Logos is reasoning, logical argument, or **content**. This is where raw information like facts and evidence are used logically, to make a convincing argument. In "The Art of Arguing" (chapter 2 in the debating section of this book), there is a lot more detail about being logical.

Together, these are the three qualities that make a speech appeal to an audience. They need to be present in every speech you make, but you mix them up differently and emphasise one over another, depending on the type of speech it is. It's a bit like cooking. The same ingredients can be used in different ways to produce different results. Also like cooking, it's the finished product that's of interest. No one says, "Great flour in this cake!" They just enjoy the cake. No one's likely to say, "Good logical reasoning in that speech, from a highly credible speaker with great audience connection," because the Pillars of Public Speaking are hidden from view. They'll know it was a great speech, though.

SIX THINGS TO THINK ABOUT WHEN PREPARING TO SPEAK

I know six is a lot of things, so we'll break them into two groups of three. You need to consider both groups as you get your speech ready. They will help you decide what to say and how to say it.

The first group is the **three major speech types**. Most public speaking is intended to **inform**, **persuade**, or **entertain** (or some combination of the three). Each of these requires slightly different content and a different presentation style. By deciding which one of the three approaches is most suitable, and combining and balancing them, you'll make speeches people remember.

The second group, **purpose**, **setting**, and **audience**, concerns the situation you are in. A good speaker adjusts their message to the audience and the situation.

The art of public speaking involves all six of these. They swirl around and blend together and you have a lot of freedom in the way you use them.

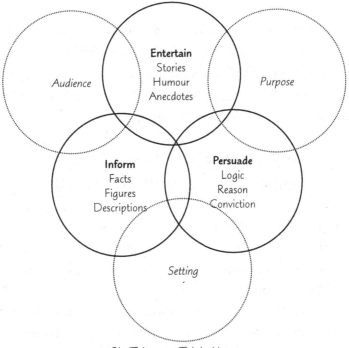

Entertain
Stories
Humour
Anecdotes

Audience

Purpose

Inform
Facts
Figures
Descriptions

Persuade
Logic
Reason
Conviction

Setting

Six Things to Think About

Inform

Informative speeches convey the facts — not much more. Updates, announcements, and class presentations are examples of speeches that inform the audience.

Perhaps you are reporting the sports results, or telling classmates the evacuation procedure, or letting people know where the buses will be for tomorrow's field trip. Maybe you are doing an in-class report on a science experiment or project.

Your big problem with an informative speech is the dryness of the material. Facts, facts, facts … It's easy to find yourself in Dullsville, and then people don't listen. An info-heavy speech will need livening up, no matter what the subject. A dollop of entertainment is going to be required. Find the human interest angle. Tell a story whenever you can. Personalize what you say.

For example, if you're announcing the sports scores, name the person most improved, or a person who did something remarkable. Comment on how the teams are doing overall. Congratulate individuals or a group and don't forget the coach.

My school had a brilliantly funny prefect who announced the sport results each week at assembly. His deadpan recounts of the action and hilarious player nicknames brought the house down every single week. He transformed the most challenging of speaking jobs into the item everyone loved to hear.

Persuade

Persuasion means to convince or get someone to do something you want them to do. Persuasion is the magic ingredient in "vote for me," "please support," or "help needed" speeches. Anything that wants the audience to change their beliefs or attitudes, or do something different, is trying to persuade.

In fact, most speeches are at least a bit persuasive. We want people to take our side whether we're telling them about our hobbies or that we want something — the items on our Christmas present list, for instance, or an extension on an assignment.

To be persuasive, you need to give a reason for the audience to do what you want. Emotional appeal as well as logic will be your tools. You need to give them the facts, some reasons why this is the best or the right thing to do, and an idea of what action to take.

For example: "I know you all think that collecting for the Red Cross is a good thing to do, but my job is to help you see that this Sunday it is what you *must* do. You can be one of the thousands of young people who can be proud of giving help to people in need. When you're older, you can donate your blood or your money. But for now, we just want some of your time. We'll take your names as you leave the hall."

Let's say you are talking on an environmental topic. Think about the impression you'll create if you are light-hearted, or serious, or dramatic, or outraged (to mention just a few of the options). Depending on the situation and your intention, any of these could either help or hinder what you want to communicate.

Entertain

Speeches at celebrations and special occasions can be a really big moment for a speaker. You can make (or break) the event. Maybe it's a toast, congratulations, or a birthday, wedding, anniversary, or award ceremony. These occasions often mark a change or achievement in someone's life or the beginning or end of something. This style of speech uses your personality and sense of humour and needs lots of connection between you and your listeners. You want it to be a feel-good experience. Some general guidelines:

- Emphasize the things that everyone present can share in.

- Use language that your audience understands. (Sometimes students use terms that are meaningful at their own school but would confuse a guest.)
- Don't make mean jokes or tell embarrassing stories.
- Find a way of saying, "We all belong here and here are some things that we share."

Let's say you make a winning speech about something that concerns your school. Now you're a regional finalist and you have to compete in front of an audience from outside your own area. Will that speech work in this setting? What if you win and have to speak in front of a national audience? And suppose you win THAT and go and speak in front of an international audience? Are they going to want to hear the same speech you made in your hometown? Probably not.

The second group of three things concerns the situation and how you fit into it.

A good speaker adjusts what they say and fits their **purpose** to the **setting** and the **audience**. This should not surprise you. You already know that you change the way you speak depending on who you're with and where you are. You don't tell your grandmother what happened at the bus stop in quite the same way you'd tell a friend.

This is fine. The way you express yourself *should* change in response to different situations. That's the mark of a good communicator.

Clarify Your Purpose

Are you clear about *why* you are speaking? What purpose does this speech serve?

Try to answer the three questions below. It may take a while, and as you work on the speech, it may change. Don't rush it.

1. Why are you doing this? What is the aim?
2. What should the audience remember after you've finished?
3. What mix of the three speech types (inform/persuade/entertain) will best get all of this across in the given situation?

Defining your purpose sounds easy, but there could be lots of options. It isn't enough to have the goal "present the findings of my science project" or "wish Jared a happy birthday." State your purpose in detail; for example, "My purpose is to make sure the class knows that even a tiny amount of salt in the soil will kill plants"; or "I want my audience to know that Jared is my best friend and he is kind and funny and I want him to feel appreciated by us all on his special day."

Consider the Setting

When you prepare your speech, you need to think about the place, the occasion, and the way you can best fit into it. Presenting a report in a classroom to your friends and speaking to family and your sister's friends at her eighteenth birthday party are very different situations. What is going to work best for you? The answer to that depends on the next two things.

Tune In to Your Audience

Let's face it: listeners are selfish. The only thing on their minds is "What's in this for me?" If the answer is "Not much," soon they'll be checking their phones or thinking about something else.

How can you make them interested enough to pay attention to you?

It's like that old cliché about walking a mile in someone else's shoes. Lots of miscommunication happens every day because the person speaking and the person listening are disconnected. A good speaker can wear the

> A speaker needs to adjust what they say to the setting and the audience. Put yourself in their position and imagine what you'd like to hear if you were where they are. Doing this helps you connect to them easily — the mark of a good communicator.

audience's shoes. Be nice to them — think about what's going to please them. You need to build rapport. Even if there are very few connections, that's an important clue as to how you should approach the task — it tells you that you need to work hard to create the links that are essential for your message to get through.

There are dozens of questions that can help you focus on the audience; for example: who are they? Why are they here? What do they need from you? What's on their minds? What are they expecting? What do they know about the topic? What do they know about you? How will they be feeling?

One of the easiest ways to connect to an audience is to admire them. Thank them for inviting you; say what a special day or place this is. Tell them something good about themselves.

One of the easiest ways to win an audience over is to admire them. Tell them something good about themselves. There's no limit to the amount of flattery people can take!

I once ran public speaking workshops after dinner for grade ten boys in a boarding school. I didn't have much experience with grade ten boys (or boarders, for that matter). And no way had they ever thought about learning public speaking. I didn't know what would be on their minds, but I was pretty sure it would not be "Fantastic! Public speaking with Ms. Duffy tonight!" I imagined them grumbling as they pulled on their sweats, "What are they making us do NOW?"

I was worried about how to break the ice, but it turned out they were just as nervous as I was. I admired their school and said what a great set-up this was and asked them a few questions about themselves. "What was on the menu tonight? How was it? Where are you from? Been boarding long? What else am I keeping you from this evening? I'm sure there's somewhere you'd rather be ..." Soon we'd had a bit of a laugh and there was enough of a connection to get down to the business of learning to make a speech in public.

Thinking about your listeners in advance will help you meet your audience's needs: the true communicator's gift.

 NOW YOU KNOW You've now got some good reasons to do public speaking, plus some tips on how to manage the nerves that are likely to bother you. You have tools to help you build a good connection with your audience, to speak in a way that is enjoyable and believable for your listeners, and to present in a way that suits the occasion and the subject.

10

How to Prepare a Speech

In this chapter you're going to learn a process for getting a speech ready. Be patient. A good speech can take a long time (days or weeks) to prepare. Before you begin to plan the exact words, you need to know what *sorts* of things to say and work out the best "angles" for this occasion and that subject. A good speech requires a lot of thought.

My advice at this early stage is simple: switch the computer off.

It is not okay to start out by writing the words. That's like building a house before you've drawn up the plans or heading out on a car trip without knowing the route — you'll go the wrong way, get lost, develop material you can't use, and waste time making avoidable corrections.

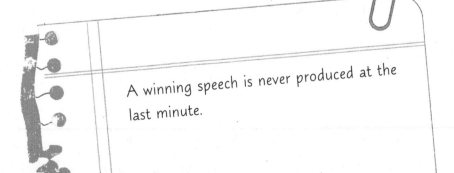

A winning speech is never produced at the last minute.

1. RESEARCH YOUR SUBJECT

Ideas for speeches come from all sorts of places ... something someone told you, an experience (yours or someone else's), something you studied in school or found out about in some other way.

If it grabbed *your* attention and made *you* think, it will do that for someone else. The important thing is that you're talking about something that matters to you.

Research stimulates new ideas and gives you a line of thought. It's like going diving and poking around whatever you find. Start by exploring your area of interest. Keep an open mind. Be prepared to change tack as you discover something new and exciting.

2. FIND THE KEY IDEAS

Ask yourself three questions:

1. What is most important/special/memorable about this issue/topic/occasion?
2. What is the main thing that the others attending should know/feel/understand?
3. What should happen as a result of my talk?

To help get to the bottom of the first question, think back to when the subject was new to you, too:

- What surprised or interested you most? Why?
- What do you understand now that you didn't before?
- Is there anything new or unexpected involved?
- Were there any lightbulb moments or funny episodes that stick in your mind?

Just about anything that made you feel interested will work the same way on your audience. Pretend you're talking about it to a friend. What would you tell them about your science project or about Jared's birthday? What would they ask you? What would they want to know?

3. DECIDE ON THE "TAKE-AWAY MESSAGE"

You should come up with a STAR, which stands for **Something They'll Always Remember**. In any presentation, people probably recall only one major message. What do you want that one thing to be?

Every day in newsrooms, editors decide which story leads the bulletin; they write a headline to work like a magnet, attracting the audience. Be like one of those editors. Convert the purpose of your speech into one message that a listener will take away from your talk. Write it down. You may or may not use exactly those words in your talk, but you will be guided by what they mean.

4. DEVELOP THE SCRIPT

Hold on! Don't switch the computer on yet. Here's a process to follow first.

Five-Step Brain Dump

1. On separate bits of paper, Post-it notes, or cue cards, write down (in note form) the facts, bright ideas, thoughts, and opinions that have jumped into your mind on this subject. One idea per card or Post-it. If you have too many, that's good!
2. Sort these into issues or themes that relate to each other. Look at your material and see what "families" suggest themselves.
3. Create headings for each of these groups.
4. Sort them into "must say" and "could say." Throw out the ones that don't fit well.
5. See if what remains can be grouped into three "chapters" (which is a satisfying and reliable structure). Do you have enough/too much/too little material for the time you have to fill? The section on page 235 on "Timing and Length" has more on this, but you'll need about seven hundred words of text for a five-minute speech. Looking at the notes you now have, try and guess whether you are going to need to expand or cut back.

Arranging the Parts

Now you need to sort the ideas into a sensible structure. But how exactly should you put those pieces together? What goes where?

The order in which you present your material gives the listener a sense of shape and direction. Choosing the right basic pattern depends on what you want to achieve, how much time you have, and what you like.

Believe it or not, you already know many of the available patterns. In a movie, you know the chase scene means the end is near; if the hero is in a cave with his enemy, the rescue party is about to turn up. You've been sensing the tension building and releasing, driving toward a conclusion we unconsciously know to be there. You recognize the pattern.

Here are the most commonly used patterns. Always choose what suits your material and the audience best.

- **Chronological or past/present/future:** good for sequencing, but it must tell a story, not just deliver a list.
- **Compare and contrast:** considers two or more options and looks for the similarities and also their differences.
- **Problem/solution:** describes a current problem or harm and sets out a way to overcome it.
- **Cause-effect:** explains how and why something has occurred.

When you've chosen a basic arrangement, put the Post-its in the right order. What you've done is "storyboard" your speech. At this point, leave it to sit and simmer. When you return to it in a few hours or days, you may make some changes. Keep doing this till you are confident you have everything there that you want and that it's been arranged in a good working order. Then *and only then* should you start to write the words of your speech.

Beginnings, Middles, and Ends

Now it's time to develop and connect the ideas on your Post-it notes. Here are the major body parts of any speech.

Introduction

Heard of "the sizzling start"? The audience's attention is highest at the start, so get it and keep it. Here is where you can use surprising facts, rhetorical questions, unexpected information, a joke, or story. ("Hey, Ma — wait'll you hear THIS!")

Make them curious. Imagine if a murder mystery began with an announcement of whodunnit. Not going to work!

Because it's so important, the opening should be one of the last things you decide on and polish up.

Background

This gives the audience any explanations or information they need to understand what's coming next.

Development

This is the main body of the speech. It's usually where you do most of your writing work. It's okay to write the introduction, background, and conclusion *after* you have developed a good solid body for the speech.

THE RULE OF THREE

For some reason that we can't quite explain, it's easy to remember three things. If you have three things to say, it sounds complete, whole, and compelling. (See what I mean?) With one or two points, you may not be quite so memorable. (See again?) With more than three points, you risk being a bore. Three points — treated fully with PREP (see page 120) — are enough for any speech. Think of each point as a chapter.

You can let it rip. Say what you want to say. If you are a funny person, bring out the tall stories and jokes. Show the audience a good time. Top it up with examples and evidence — an audience visibly sits up and pays attention when they hear the words "for example ..." so make sure you use plenty of them. And tell stories — people love stories.

Conclusion

This draws everything together gracefully in a summary and finalises it in a simple, memorable way. It's the "call to action" point, where you can state what you want the audience to do, if that's part of your plan.

There are a number of standard endings that you can use. For example:

- **Bookending** — this is when you work your way back to your opening or title. This has a nicely balanced feel to it.
- **Challenging or inviting** your audience to do something.
- **Closing with a famous quote** or reference that everyone will know.

The "speech house" illustration below shows you how the different parts of a speech fit together.

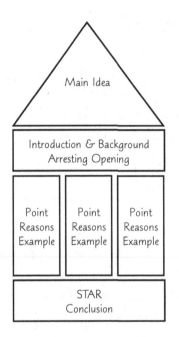

The "Speech House"

There is one idea over the top, like a roof. After your set-up remarks, there are three separate "chapters" that make up the body of the speech. Each has a well-developed "point, reason, example" structure. Finally you draw it all together gracefully, with some concluding remarks and something they'll always remember.

Sample Speech Outline

Let's say your speech is about waste disposal (by which I mean sewage). You've chosen a problem/solution structure. Here's an outline of what you could say.

How to Prepare a Speech

Main Idea   The sewage system is more important than you know, and less appreciated than it should be.

Sizzling Start Option 1: The average person makes a ton of poo every year. Option 2: Guess how much poo we each make a year?

Problem   As cities grow, all this defecating puts a pressure on the aging waste disposal system. (Tell them when the sewage system in your city was installed and when it had its last upgrade). Those pipes are groaning and stretching and cracking after decades of hard work. If they break, the consequences will be terrible. I'm talking about disease — never mind the bad smells. Really nasty illnesses that people die from are spread when there's no safe sewage system. The pipes need to be replaced every few decades, but sewage projects are disruptive and costly, and as the system is hidden down deep beneath the streets, it's easy to pay no attention until something goes disastrously wrong. (Example) The 2011 Christchurch, New Zealand, earthquake destroyed 80 percent of the city's sewer infrastructure. With no pipes, there is no sanitation. Ick.

Solution   Get citizens to understand the importance of the sewer upgrades so they'll accept the inconvenience and the cost.

For example, in San Francisco, a creative public information campaign, with ads on buses all about poop and pee, was the talk of the town. It was funny and effective, because everybody could relate to it. They were glad to see the new sewers being installed.

STAR   Sanitation stinks but without it public health is in peril. Save our sewers!

5. WRITE THE DRAFT

Speaking and Writing — The Difference

We speak in ways we would never write and write in ways we would never speak. One of the biggest mistakes for a speaker is to think of a speech as something you write. It's not. A speech is *spoken*. It's a LIIIIIVE gig. The key to speaking success is being good to *listen* to.

A speech is happening now. The spoken word is conversational. We use it to express how we feel, what we want, what we're thinking about. The written word exists beyond the here and now. It uses a different vocabulary. Written language can be complex; readers put up with longer words and sentences and wanderings around the point. Writing has commas and parentheses and all sorts of features that, when spoken, make a speech sound fake, stagy, and pompous. Try reading this paragraph aloud and you will see what I mean.

What you say needs to sound natural. You need your own style, but it must work in the world of the spoken word. A speech is not an essay-out-loud.

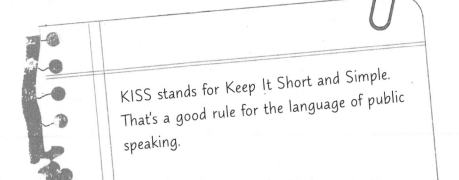

KISS stands for Keep It Short and Simple. That's a good rule for the language of public speaking.

To hear the difference between speaking and writing, notice the words you use in conversation. I bet you use short words and sentences, and you're direct and straightforward. Lively. Vivid, even. This is what we want.

Keep it simple, and people will find it much easier to listen to you.

The different sections of your speech should be linked by phrases that act as signposts to take the listener easily from one part to the next, as if they were going along a pathway; for example, "Let's talk about …" or "Now we have to consider the other side of the question …"

Timing and Length

You need to time yourself reading aloud to learn how many words you speak per minute. Then you can calculate the length of your script. As a very rough guide, about seven hundred words turns into five speaking minutes, though this varies a lot from person to person.

MS. DUFFY'S TOP TIP
Start with loads of words on your cards, then rewrite as you practise out loud. The better you know your speech, the fewer words you will need.

What if I told you that chocolate has a dark, dark past, (1)
its roots buried way back in ancient civilizations?

What if I told you a chocolate drink was served as a last
comfort to human sacrifice victims, and the beans it
was made from were once smeared with the blood
of a high Aztec priest?

What if I told you each bite contained over 300
chemicals — mood improvers, energizers, and
stimulants?

What if I told you African children work for a pittance
in slave-like conditions to produce it, without even
knowing what it is?

Would you still want to eat it if you really knew what it's
doing to you and what it's done to others?

- - - -

In fact, it started out as a health food.

(2)

Way back in history the Aztecs and Mayans of (3)
Central Mexico drank a bitter-tasting drink
made of ground cacao beans mixed with chilli
and pepper,

which they thought was a kind of magical cure-all,
thought to fix diarrhea and dysentery, to confer
wisdom, and to be an aphrodisiac.

When chocolate was brought to Europe, doctors
used the "miracle drink" to

Whole Speech on Cards

(4)

- fight weight gain
- stimulate the nervous system
- improve digestion
  and to treat
- anaemia
- mental fatigue
- tuberculosis
- fever and gout
- kidney stones ... and even to aid childbirth.

Once you're sure you've written a well-structured
speech, you need to speak it aloud and time it. Change
anything that tangles up your lips and tongue. Delete
or add words so you come in bang on time. If you can't
deliver a prepared speech in exactly the time allotted,
you are not going to impress anyone.

Cue Cards and Scripts

When you're sure the script is finalized, put it on cue cards. You can write the whole speech out word for word, but it's better if you can just use trigger words and phrases. Practise using the cards. You need to be able to find your way to the next point after you've looked up at the audience. You MUST NUMBER the cards.

If your speech is staying on a piece of paper, use 14-point type and double-space it. That makes it easy to read when you glance at it. Put some key words in bold so you can easily find them when you glance down.

If your notes are on a lectern, slide your finger or a pen down the page as you progress so you don't lose your place when you look up at the audience and down again at the words.

6. REHEARSE
(OR WHY YOU SHOULD PRACTISE YOUR SPEECH TILL YOU WOULD RATHER DO ANYTHING ELSE)

Delivering a speech unrehearsed is like doing a piano exam without practising or handing in the first draft of an essay. You'd be an idiot to turn up to a championship game without any training, yet some people think they can speak in public without any rehearsal.

A band has lots of rehearsals and a final soundcheck to give the performers confidence that everything in the show works. A speech should be approached in the same way. Aim to become familiar enough with your script that you know your way around it but not so overprepared that your zing fades and you sound stale. For a "big deal" speech, this usually means rehearsing several times a day, then dropping off as the event approaches.

Record yourself. You can use the video on a smartphone or the voice memo feature if you don't want to watch yourself. When you play the recording back, it will be easy to decide what works. Re-record and repeat as often as you have to, until you are happy with your performance. This might take you five attempts; it might take fifty. Just persist. Most people are their own harshest critics, so take it easy ... you are probably better than you think!

The very best thing you can do is rehearse under pressure. Speak in front of an audience: your family, your friends, or (better still) people you don't know. Their responses will build your confidence, and their reactions may even guide you to make changes in what you had planned to say.

Rehearsal helps you keep to time. It helps you get used to looking up and out at the audience, so that you don't get locked into looking down at your notes. It also helps you keep a calm exterior when the nerves strike. Your lips, teeth, tongue, and brain are unlikely to all desert you all at once if you've run through the speech a few times in advance. This is called "muscle memory" — you're teaching your mouth to remember your speech for you.

Rehearsal gives you time to edit and rearrange what you will say. Hearing yourself out loud will highlight areas that need to be changed. Your script is only final when you've tidied everything up and know you will talk to the time limit.

When you're confident about what to say and about your timing, you're free to focus on your audience and respond to them. You can stop worrying about the basics and instead work with the room and keep your presentation dynamic and alive.

NOW YOU KNOW Public speaking is about being worth listening to. In this section we've looked in detail at how to prepare a speech.

- You have a process for deciding what to say and organizing your material so that the speech is interesting.
- You know how to develop a script that will not sound like an essay-out-loud.
- You've got advice for rehearsing to give you confidence and to help you fine tune.

11

You're On!

In this section we look at the physical practicalities of speaking so you can be smooth and polished when you do what you have to do in front of an audience.

MAKING THE MOST OF YOUR VOICE

A speaker's voice is their main tool. Voice is every bit as important as looks, charm, and intelligence when it comes to making a good impression. In the first few seconds you are speaking, any listener will unconsciously make a judgement about you based partly on the way you sound.

A voice is like a paintbrush for words. It puts meaning into your text. You can use it to underline and emphasize, to show light and shade. You can vary the pitch, volume, pace, and tone of your voice, as well as the type of language you use, to engage your audience and bring your speech to life.

Each voice is distinctive, with its own colour and texture. You were born with your voice, and you can't grow a new one or change it completely, but you can make the best use of it.

Who do you like to listen to? Just for fun, try to mimic the patterns of their speech and feel what it is they do. I bet their voice is melodious, resonant, pleasing to the ear. They have clear diction; their voice carries. They speak at a pace that is easy to follow, and if they speak at length, they do so with enough variety to be interesting.

What about your voice? Do you speak fluently or stop and start a lot? Do you mumble or mash your words together, or do you speak clearly? When you're under pressure are you a quick talker or a slow and deliberate one? Record yourself and replay it. You will learn a lot.

Language and Tone

These must fit the occasion. Generally, in public speaking you need to be clear and direct and a bit more "proper" than in ordinary conversation. One trick is to imagine you are talking to an older person, like a grandparent or teacher. That will put you in the right language mode. Slang is not a good idea. Swearing is right out.

Volume and Pace

This is pretty obvious, but a speaker must be heard to be understood. In a big space you'll need a microphone or to PROJECT. A voice bounces around and echoes in a large space like an assembly hall or a church, so speak s-l-o-w-l-y, or what you say will turn to mush because of the reverberation.

Practise filling a large space without shouting. Get a friend to stand outside the room and talk to her or him. See how much more distinctly and slowly you have to speak? You need to work your lips, teeth, and tongue quite a bit harder than normally.

For public speaking, you will almost certainly need to speak slower than you do in private. It feels weird but sounds fine.

Pitch and Clarity

These must work for you. If your voice is naturally high, or soft, or hard to understand for some other reason (for example, braces can disturb your articulation, or you might have a lisp or another disfluency), you need to know this so you can work around it. Generally, a strong, medium-paced, medium- to low-pitched voice is what a listener likes to hear.

POISE ON THE PODIUM

Stagecraft is part of the presentation. Where does the speech happen? Where do you enter and exit? Where do you wait or sit and stand? Do you have a lectern to use? Are you going to use a microphone?

Before You Speak

Get there early and study the set-up. Go into the space and check it out. Hop into the spot you'll speak from and see how it feels. What are the sight lines like? Can you see everyone? What about the lighting? Is your face illuminated or in shadow? Can you see your audience (important for eye contact)? Remember that stage lighting may blind you, and the audience may be in darkness. If you can't happily speak without seeing your audience (and who can?), ask for the house lights to go up.

The Technology

If you are going to use it, technology needs to be checked, double-checked, and triple-checked. You don't want to have your presentation ruined by some simple adjustments that you could have taken care of beforehand.

Check the height of the microphone. Will you have to raise or lower it? Switch it on and speak — how do you sound? Is there a reverb? Are you popping or hissing? Where are your AV controls? Where do you put your notes?

Getting On and Off

Where will you enter and exit? If you're going up stairs to get on stage, do it with your body erect and your head up as much as possible. Don't run or jump or take two stairs at a time. Don't rush — just move purposefully.

If you have to carry anything with you, work out how you'll keep it tidy and not drop it.

Being seated properly in public means your knees and ankles are close together, and there's a pleasant expression on your face. Stay still. Don't fidget or put your hands to your face or hair. Don't communicate in any way with anyone in the audience, and remember, everyone can see you. Don't look at your shoes — it makes you look bored.

When You're On

Be confident — look at your audience and smile at them when you arrive at your speaking position.

When there's applause or laughter, pause and wait for it to subside before you continue.

After Speaking

Don't walk away the second you finish. Count "one, two" silently and then make your exit. Eyes up, steady pace as before.

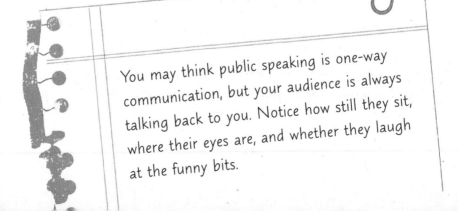

You may think public speaking is one-way communication, but your audience is always talking back to you. Notice how still they sit, where their eyes are, and whether they laugh at the funny bits.

If you have to move around on stage, you should stay out of the way of others. For example, if you get an award, shake hands with the giver and move out of the way so the next person can come forward.

Sometimes, like at award ceremonies, you need to have a photo taken. Stay collected and stand still, smile for the photographer, wait a moment, then move on.

Appearance

Keep it neat, please! You don't want the audience to be distracted by ties undone and shirts untucked. And frankly, these look sloppy. If you're not in uniform, wear something that feels neat and suits the occasion.

Body Language

Stand in a relaxed position, without swaying (a common nervous habit) or hanging on to the lectern. Plant your feet, as if your legs were trees. This makes you feel solid and conveys authority.

Have your arms loosely by your sides, your feet hip-width apart — it's narrower then you think. Drop your shoulders and stick your chest out. You may feel like folding your arms, lowering your head, or putting your hands in your pockets — that's because your fight-or-flight chemicals are telling you to hide. Don't. You may feel better, but you'll look much worse.

Don't clench anything visible: teeth, shoulders, fists. You can screw your toes up inside your shoes if it helps.

Turn squarely to face a person and look them in the eye when you shake their hand.

Smile. Smiling helps in two ways, relaxing your mind and your body.

Gestures should arise naturally from what you say. You'll look stilted if they look planned or artificial, so make sure you can be "spontaneous" when you use your arms or hands to enhance what you are saying. The further you are from your audience, the bigger your gestures will have to be. Avoid empty gestures like bouncing and hand flapping, though. These are really an inability to conquer your nerves enough to keep still.

Depending on the occasion and how long you're speaking for, you might plan and write some stage directions to yourself in your speech notes — "shrug shoulders," "pause," and so on — and underline the words you want to emphasise.

Eye Contact

Eye contact with the audience is most important, whether you're in a classroom or addressing a crowd of a thousand. Looking away from your audience makes them feel as though you're avoiding them. Looking at them makes them feel included.

In the speaker-audience relationship, you are the leader. Keep your eyes travelling through the audience, stopping to look straight at different people as you speak.

Cover all sections of the room. Don't ignore one side or the other or look to the front of the audience without looking to the back of the room. Write a note in your speech text; for example, "LOOK REAR, LOOK LEFT."

Be sure to look directly at individuals. If you really can't look directly at people, then float your eyes just above their heads. Or if going eyeball-to-eyeball is too scary, gaze at their eyebrows instead.

Somehow Hannah always had trouble connecting with people.

Lecterns

A lectern can be a protective barrier and a place to put your notes. It adds dignity to a formal or religious occasion. Some speakers cling to a lectern as if it will save their life. The biggest problem for young speakers is that the lectern can be taller than you are. Get yourself something to stand on and don't lean or hunch into the microphone. It's there to serve you, not the other way round. Adjust it so it's the right height. Your audience won't mind if you take a minute to prepare the space before you start to speak.

Microphones

Microphones come in several types. The first clips to your lapel or collar. It has a battery pack, which you wear at your waistband. A lapel mic lets you speak normally, with the same amount of volume and vocal projection you would use to address a small group. The amplifier will do the rest.

A mic can be attached to a stand or podium. You don't need to eat it. It's designed to pick your voice up from up to thirty centimetres away, so don't hunch over it, lean into it, or alter your body shape to get your mouth closer to it. You should speak OVER these mics, not into them.

You might have a hand-held mic. The rules are much the same as for mics on a stand. Keep it a hand's-width or so away from your mouth. Holding something in front of your face like this might feel awkward, but the mic mustn't sag down to waist height — at least, not if you want to be heard. If you have notes, you'll need to hold them in the other hand and out to the side.

With this type of microphone, popping can be a problem. Popping is caused when the letters "p," "t," and "d" are spoken and the air from your mouth hits the mic. To prevent popping, position the mic about a hand's-width away and slightly below your mouth so that the air from your mouth does not hit the microphone. Blowing in any microphone (including the one in your cellphone) can damage it and also hurts the ears of the listener.

Mics can screech and whoop and give you feed-back, which completely ruins the experience for you and those listening to you. If you have rehearsed in advance, you should have a feel for how to best posi-tion the mic to avoid this. If something does go wrong during your presentation, wait for the rescue party — the IT person or the person in charge. They can sort it out. Then calmly start again. If time is pressing or the mic can't be fixed for some reason, switch it off, step aside, and just speak up.

Always remember that a microphone is LIVE. Don't say anything you don't want the world to hear. Even if you think it's switched off, it's best not to risk saying that funny little joke to yourself in front of the mic!

NOW YOU KNOW "Stagecraft" is an essential part of presenting yourself well. In this section we've looked at how to stay calm and collected (and how to look it even if you don't feel it), how to make the best use of your voice, how to look poised on the podium, and how to deal with lights, mics, and lecterns with a polished presentation.

12

Speech Making
in Real Life

We're now going to take a look at how to prepare for real-life public speaking situations in more detail.

At school, you are likely to have quite a few opportunities to speak in public, either in class, at school events, or in interschool competitions. You might speak at

- a public speaking competition;
- assembly, giving the sports results and announcing upcoming events;
- an awards ceremony, reading names aloud, or even presenting or receiving an award;
- student elections — a "vote for me" speech or acceptance speech;
- an occasion where you introduce and thank a guest; or
- in church, doing a reading.

PUBLIC SPEAKING COMPETITIONS

Competitions are a great way to test your skills. Competitive public speaking is very different from debating and from the other speaking tasks that school students do.

There are competitions at all age levels, depending on where you are and what type of school you attend. Your school enters you for these. As the number of students who can go into these competitions is limited, the standard can be very high. If you do well, you may find yourself representing your region, state/province, or even your country, as you progress successfully through every level.

Most regional education departments run competitions, and there are also many smaller local competitions organized by clubs like Rotary or Lions or by churches and other community-based organizations like cadets. Individual schools often have their own speaking award or competition as well.

If you are entering a competition, check what exactly the organizers are looking for. Study the guidelines. Below are some possible variations:

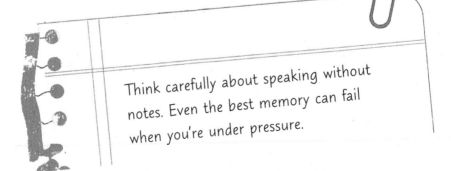

Think carefully about speaking without notes. Even the best memory can fail when you're under pressure.

- Some competitions set the topics. Usually these are general or metaphorical; for example, *A light bulb moment* or *The tide has turned*. The idea is to leave you free to make a speech that relates to the topic in some way, but where you choose how you will interpret it.
- Some let you choose your own topic.
- Some have a general theme — for example, that the speech should be consistent with the values of the organization running the competition — but, again, you are free to work out exactly how to achieve that.
- Some like you to memorize the speech; some like you to use notes or cards.
- Some want an impromptu speech as well as the prepared speech.

Competitive public speaking rewards a combination of skills. The way you deliver the speech is just as important as what you say. The speech should be original — you can offer a personal, fresh new view of something. Don't rehash what someone else thinks; think for yourself instead. Use your own life experience and brainpower to explore an issue in a way that only you can. Don't just give a recount, though — you must have a purpose, some new insight. There does need to be a point!

One of the most memorable speeches I ever judged was by a ten-year-old boy on the topic *My Family*. His

Be ready for anything and everything
to go wrong! BRING A SPARE
COPY OF EVERYTHING.

parents were foster carers. His talk was about how much he loved it when a new baby came into the house; how sweet they were, and how he liked changing the diapers, and holding them, and having cuddles and tickles and fun. He made us see that his family was very special. It was a simple, personal speech about ordinary things, but it was his own story, told well, and it had a lot to say about what matters.

To prepare a speech for a competition you should follow the process in chapter 10. Allow plenty of time to get it ready. A winning speech is never produced at the last minute!

IMPROMPTU SPEAKING — TIPS FOR THINKING ON YOUR FEET

In some competitions, you have to make an impromptu or off-the-cuff speech as well as your prepared speech.

MS. DUFFY'S TOP TIP

In a competition, always present your impromptu speech on a different topic and in a different style from your prepared speech. This shows the judge you are a versatile speaker. If you were serious in one, be light in the other. Steer clear of anything you've already said — don't recycle information.

You are given a topic and a very short time to prepare your speech. *The impromptu speech may count as much as the prepared speech.*

Many students can deliver a good prepared speech, but impromptu speaking is pretty intimidating. It scares even top-notch speakers. It's public-speaking anxiety Big Time.

If you find yourself needing to speak with very little preparation time, here are some techniques to help you.

Your Point?

You need to have something to say. Sounds easy; isn't easy. Like all speeches, your impromptu speech needs to make a point. Don't just start telling a story and hoping for the best. Know where you're going. Once you are underway, you can't stop and think.

Prepare in Advance

Many speakers prepare a stock of fun facts and anecdotes and some good opening and closing lines. These are like files to download if they fit the impromptu topic.

Preparing a pile of things you could say is a good idea. However, do not precook a whole speech and just change the title. It's very obvious when students do this, and it undermines the purpose of the impromptu speech task. Use your "files" as if they were Lego pieces. Mix and build them to fit the topic.

Start at the Finish

You should start by preparing your final few words. Know where you are going to land, and you can fly through the speech to get there. Having a destination in mind gives you direction. You can then open with a comment or anecdote or a piece of information that you return to at the close of the speech.

Just One Idea

Keep it moving. Don't start with one sentence and then change direction, go off-course, or go off on a tangent. You must travel from the beginning to the end of your speech in a purposeful and polished way.

Use a Framework

Here are three easy frameworks:

1. **PREP (point, reason, example, point):** Make
   your point. Elaborate and give a reason (or reasons,
   if you have more time). Give an example and,
   finally, finish by restating the main point, using
   different words so it's not repetitive.
2. **Pros versus cons:** Start off by explaining an
   issue. Talk about its good side and then talk
   about the downside. Finish by offering your own
   opinion.
3. **Who, what, when, where, and why?:** Identify an
   issue, then explore it using these different angles.
   Reach a conclusion of some sort.

What the Judges Are Looking For

There may be specific criteria for particular competitions. In general, the judge is looking for a speaker with a natural, genuine style, whose voice, body, and words work together to create interest, convey a message, and make a good connection with the audience.

Of course, a speaker should also be audible, clear, confident, and on top of the subject. Original ideas and imaginative and varied use of language are usually rewarded.

Here are the criteria I use when I'm judging:

- **Subject, reasoning, and evidence:** The point of the speech is very clear. Ideas flow in a logical structure, with convincing evidence and examples.
- **Creative thinking:** Original, creative, and unusual ideas and perspectives are offered.
- **Structure — opening and closing:** The opening is arresting and maintains attention. The speech has a climax — the audience is left with a definite conclusion, or take-away message, or call to action.
- **Expression and delivery:** The speaker has a natural, genuine style with good eye contact. He or she is audible and confident. Notes are used to support and don't interfere with the speaker's delivery.
- **Language:** The speaker uses imaginative and varied use of language and style (for example, wit, humour, anecdote, information, reflection) and rhetorical devices like questions, repetition, contrasting pairs, or the "rule of three."
- **Audience engagement:** The speaker's language creates strong rapport. Voice, body, and words together create interest. The audience has an emotional response.

EVENTS AND CEREMONIES

If you are in a leadership role at school you might have official duties on special occasions. Here's a quick guide to what to do on the most common of these.

Introducing a Speaker

Your job is to set up the speaker and excite the audience about what is to come. Introductions should be graceful and fun. An introduction serves two purposes:

- It gives the audience time to adjust to what's coming up.
- It prepares people for the speaker, making them feel receptive.

Your task is to introduce the speaker, not to take centre stage yourself. The spotlight belongs on them. Keep it brief. For informal gatherings, thirty seconds is plenty. For larger events, aim for no longer than a minute. Some basic guidelines:

- Take the time to prepare well before you speak. Don't put your introduction together at the last minute.
- Ask the speaker for input. Make a call in advance to ask what he or she would like to emphasize, what's especially interesting. Learn as much as you can about their experience, education, life, interests.
- Ask how to pronounce her or his name. If it's a tricky one for you, write it down phonetically and put the syllables to be stressed in capital letters; for example, Mr. Abisheganaden could be written as "Mr. a-BISH-gan-AH-den."

- Don't read your introduction out — it shows you didn't prepare.
- Add some perspective of your own. What interests you about this person? Share it.
- Thank them, be grateful that the speaker is there. Chances are they are just as nervous as you, and some warm words — for example, "We're very pleased to welcome …" — will make things easier.
- Conclude your intro with the speaker's name, which is their cue to come forward or stand up. Lead the applause as the speaker walks to the podium. Wait there until they arrive. Then step back.

Sample Introduction

It's an assembly and you're introducing the highbrow scientist who's come along to talk to the school.

Takeaway Message

(NB: This is not spoken aloud — it's the thought behind your intro.)
Dr. Zachary Spindlehead is a real hot shot and you should listen to him because he is very very famous and inspiring and funny, and he can help some of us to see scientific research in a new way.

Speech

"Grab-them" opening	"There are not many chances for a seventeen-year-old to meet a Nobel Prize winner, but you are about to get one …"

Tell the audience what to expect; give a basic professional profile, but interestingly presented	Dr. Spindlehead has a lifelong involvement with ditswack fangdoodling. It started when he found his father's fangdoodler in the back shed, at age seven. Young Zach was hooked. And has been on the fangdoodling path ever since.
	Dr. Spindlehead has been at the forefront of some important discoveries. Bloop goodling and blub glupping are two you will be familiar with.
	The grade twelves among us are facing some choices about our future, and Dr. Spindlehead's perspective on scientific research as a career is a gift we should all be grateful for.
Conclusion and handover	"I welcome Dr. Spindlehead here today." (Lead the applause as he comes forward, wait at the podium until he arrives, then move away and take your seat.)

Thanking a Speaker

To thank a speaker is a lot easier, because you have heard their speech. All you then have to do is comment on something he or she mentioned, to show that it was really worth listening to. Compliment the speech and never challenge the content. Lead a second round of applause.

Presenting an Award

It's an honour for you to speak on behalf of an organization and present an award. Greet the audience and say what an important occasion it is. After that, you need to cover the following things. You can do it in thirty seconds or a minute, depending on the event.

- Give the background to the award.
- Explain why it's your job to present it.
- Elaborate upon this person's achievements.
- Explain what they did, the difference they have made.
- Make the formal presentation.
- Lead the applause, then stand back and let the person move forward to make an acceptance speech or stand with them for the photo.

Receiving an Award

Sooner or later, you're probably going to win something. It may be a surprise, or you may have time to prepare to receive it. You need to be excited, grateful, and humble but not so humble that the audience imagines you don't think much of the honour.

Some basic guidelines for an acceptance speech:

- Keep it short.
- Be grateful and happy.
- Speak about how much the award matters.
- Praise the competition and the other competitors.
- Share the credit — mention those who made it possible for you to win the award.
- Say what the award means to you. What inspired you to do the thing you're being awarded for? Say what difference receiving this award makes to your life.
- Conclude with a final "Thank you."

Social Occasions

Graduations, weddings, birthdays, anniversaries, farewells
… all these occasions feature a speech.

As a speaker on these occasions, you should be
lively and exciting. Be funny, emotional, and personal
in the way you talk about things.

Your speech should address all the different people
in the audience. Say something about what the person or
the occasion means to you, but also look at what others
will be feeling. What would a friend, family member,
colleague, or coach want to hear? An eighteenth birthday could be spoiled for the parents and grandparents
if the speech was only from a young person's point of
view. If you're speaking about your sister, make sure you
say something about her as a friend or daughter as well.
If it's your grandparents' fiftieth wedding anniversary,
mention their old friends as well as family of all generations. A graduation speech should be relevant for the
students, their parents, families, and teachers.

You will need to research these perspectives and
speak to others to collect ideas and anecdotes.

You have to be entertaining on these occasions but
take care — jokes must be meant kindly. Don't make fun
of anyone. It is not the time for payback or stories about
"socially unacceptable" experiences. "No embarrassment,
no surprises" is a good rule for special occasion speeches.

You may be on a stage or at a microphone on the
floor. Often the audience at a party can be all around

you, so you need to be sure to include everyone with your eyes as you speak. You mustn't speak with your back to anyone, so if the organizers haven't thought of this, make sure you take a speaking position that gives you command of the whole room.

Reading Aloud in Public

Reading in public — for example, reading out a list of names at an award ceremony or a prayer in church — is one of the few occasions when the audience can know you've made a mistake, as chances are they have a program or order of service that they're following.

Be doubly sure to prepare and rehearse aloud in advance, so you pronounce everything correctly. You must use your voice for effect: expression and tone, pitch and volume, bring your reading to life. The person reading silently to themselves cannot do this. Your voice will weave magic into the words.

To read aloud, you should look at the page briefly and scan ahead, then raise your eyes and look at the audience as you speak. The normal "eye contact" rules apply (see page 246). The idea is that you're telling the audience something, not proving that you can read. It takes practice.

It is very common for readers to speed up. You must keep a steady pace.

The short pause when you look down at your script is a useful break; there's a natural-sounding pause that keeps you going at a comfortable pace.

NOW YOU KNOW In this chapter you learned simple recipes for making speeches to suit the different types of occasions you will meet as a school-aged speaker.

Speaking well gives you influence. You too can be someone worth listening to. Go forth! Good luck!

MS. DUFFY'S (COMPLETE) DEBATING CHEAT SHEET

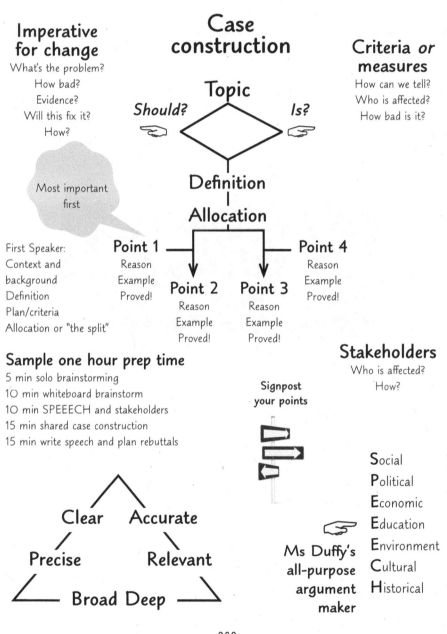

Imperative for change
What's the problem?
How bad?
Evidence?
Will this fix it?
How?

Case construction

Topic

Should? ☜   *Is?* ☞

Definition

Allocation

Criteria *or* measures
How can we tell?
Who is affected?
How bad is it?

Most important first

First Speaker:
Context and
background
Definition
Plan/criteria
Allocation or "the split"

Point 1
Reason
Example
Proved!

Point 2
Reason
Example
Proved!

Point 3
Reason
Example
Proved!

Point 4
Reason
Example
Proved!

Sample one hour prep time
5 min solo brainstorming
10 min whiteboard brainstorm
10 min SPEEECH and stakeholders
15 min shared case construction
15 min write speech and plan rebuttals

Signpost your points

Stakeholders
Who is affected?
How?

Clear   Accurate
Precise   Relevant
Broad Deep

Ms Duffy's
all-purpose
argument
maker

☞

Social
Political
Economic
Education
Environment
Cultural
Historical

ALL-PURPOSE SPEECH PLANNER

What to Do

On a separate sheet of paper

1. Brainstorm to create a mind map; e.g.:
    *   What is interesting about this?
    *   What information MUST be in it? What COULD be in it?
    *   How does it connect to your audience?
    *   What would matter out in the wider world?
    *   What is unique/curious about it?
    *   What should the audience know at the end?
2. Write down your purpose: Inform? Entertain? Persuade?
3. Write a catchy opening.
4. Write your take-away message.
5. Write your concluding sentence.
6. Turn over the page. Leave the top five centimetres blank. Now write three discussion points that will lead you from the start of your speech to the end. Number each point. Include an example for each.
7. In the blank space at the top, write the arresting opening you have planned. At the bottom of the page, insert the powerful closing you've already thought of.

Voila! A complete speech outline!

PERSUASIVE SPEECH PLAN

This "recipe" helps you to speak in a way that leads people to change their minds and hearts and agree with you. It's based on the work of a psychologist called John Monroe. It's known as Monroe's Motivated Sequence.

Persuasive Speaking — Five Steps to Success

1. Attention-Getter

Grab their attention and arouse their interest. Start with a story, example, dramatic statistic, quotation, etc.

2. State the Issue/Need

Describe the situation. Make it sound significant — a problem that is causing harm and won't go away by itself. Convince your audience that there is a need for action. Use facts and data. Your audience needs to feel they will be personally affected if they do nothing.

3. Satisfaction — Provide a Solution

Tell them how to go about fixing this problem. Make sure your solution exactly fits the problem you described in step 2.

4. Visualize the Change

Paint a word picture of the new world after your plan has been carried out. How lovely and happy we all will be!

5. Action — What They Should Do

Tell them what action they can personally take to solve the problem. Show how. It needs to be easy, immediate, and doable.

INFORMATIVE SPEECH OUTLINE

This "recipe" helps you to present information in an interesting, listenable way.

1. Clarify Your Purpose

Before you prepare the script, write down what your audience should know at the end. For example: "My purpose is to ensure that my teacher realizes that I have understood this topic in depth and can summarise it."

2. What Do They Need to Know? Why?

- List what's essential for them to hear. Is there something that's important for them to understand? Instructions they'll need to follow?
- List some reasons for listening to you. How will they be better off?

3. Build Connection with the Audience

- Think of some stories, numbers, questions — anything that will make them sit up and listen. Think about what they are wanting from you and how receptive they are. What barriers do you need to overcome to get a connection?
- Decide on what you can say to hook them in — the "sizzling start."
- Decide how you want to wind up the speech and leave them feeling satisfied.

4. Write the Speech

- Draft the body of your speech first, then the introduction and conclusion.
- Use short words and an everyday, conversational tone.
- Be clear and relevant.
- Find "human" ways to liven your facts up.

5. Satisfy Their Curiosity

Be ready for the audience to ask questions. Prepare some answers in advance so you don't get caught out.

MS. DUFFY'S FIVE-MINUTE IMPROMPTU SPEECHMAKER

What to Do

On a separate sheet of paper, or on cue cards

1. Brainstorm to create a mind map; e.g.: ⏱ 2 min
   - What comes to mind when you think of your topic?
   - Who does it matter to?
   - Any stories or incidents?
   - What is unique/curious about it?

   Write down your main aim: Inform? Entertain?
   Persuade?   ⏱ 10 sec
2. Write a catchy opening.   ⏱ 15 sec
3. Write your take-away message.   ⏱ 15 sec
4. Write your concluding sentence.   ⏱ 20 sec
5. On the reverse of the page, starting
   a few centimetres from the top,   ⏱ 2 min
   - write three points that take you from the opening to the conclusion.
   - number each point. Include an example for each.
   - add your arresting opening point at the top and your powerful closing point at the bottom.

Glossary

Adjudicator: the person who judges the debate or speaking competition.

Affirmative: the side that argues "yes" to the topic.

Allocation: who says which points. The First Proposition speaker will say, "Now for my allocation," and then give a kind of contents page for the debate: "My first point will be ... My second point will be ... My second speaker's first point will be ..." and so on.

Assertion: a point that is made but not proved with reasons. "That's just an assertion."

Case: the whole story that each team presents for their side of the topic.

Contentious: describes something that can be debated.

Debaterspeak: terms you might not encounter elsewhere. Debaters use words or phrases that other people don't, or they use them slightly differently because the context gives them a certain meaning (for example, allocation, stakeholders, the imperative for change).

Definition: the Proposition's interpretation of the topic, which explains any unclear or subjective terms. The definition says what's in and what's out of bounds.

Empirical debates: debates about what is (or is not) the case.

Examples: real-world things that provide evidence for or against a point. They could be real case studies, real countries, real laws, and so on.

Moot: describes a debateable issue. Sometimes "This is a moot point" can mean it is no longer relevant.

Negative: the side that argues "no" to the topic.

Normative: about what *should* be true, not what is true

Opposition: the side that argues "no" to the topic.

Point: a single argument. Good ones have reasons and examples and give the adjudicator and audience a reason to believe in your side of the topic.

Pre-emptive material: things you say before the other team has a chance to bring them up. You might say, "Now, I know the other team will stand up here and say that banning junk food won't improve obesity levels. Let me tell you why that's wrong."

PREP: an acronym that tells you how to make a good strong point. P — state your **point**, R — give **reasons** for believing it, E — give an **example** or some evidence, P — state what you just **proved**.

Prep: the time you have to get your case ready. Usually it's one hour.

Proposition: the side that argues "yes" to the topic.

Reasons: things that compel people to believe things. Things you need to win debates! Usually involve the word "because."

Rebuttal: a response to the other team's point (or points) that says why it's wrong. Rebuttal takes up the first part of all speeches, except for the First Proposition.

Squirrelling: university debaterspeak for deliberately misinterpreting the wording of a topic until it's undebateable.

Stakeholders: the people, groups of people, or institutions affected by a proposition — for example, teachers, children, parents, and the education system are just some of the stakeholders in a debate about changing education policy.

Status quo: Latin term that more or less means "the way things are right now."

Substantive matter: the points you use to prove your case. The opposite of rebuttal.

Thematic rebuttal: when you group your rebuttal according to themes rather than in the chronological order that the other team presented their points in.

Acknowledgements

My biggest thanks are to my daughter Eleanor, whose contributions to this book are massive. Her experience as a debater and coach is vast, and there would be no book without it. I also thank my husband, Michael, who has impressive speaking skills of his own and who gave me great advice and insights.

Next come the educators. Sandra Carter is, quite simply, a legend, a role model, and an inspiration to me and generations of her speech students. Thanks to SCEGGS Darlinghurst, where I got started in this field, and to The Scots College — especially Andrew Potter — for giving me and the debating and public speaking program unreserved support.

Students would not be doing any of this if it were not for the programs and the infrastructure that support them. Every school debating and public speaking coordinator deserves a pat on the back for their efforts. I especially want to thank Lloyd Cameron of the Arts Unit of the New South Wales Department of Education and Communities, whose leadership over many years has created an outstanding schools' speaking culture. The program fosters both participation and excellence and has had an enormous influence on thousands of school students. As a result, we have an exceptional standard of speaking.

I also want to thank all the students I've coached over the years. You are original, interesting, passionate, clever, and absolutely never dull. Spending time with you is the best job a person could wish for.